About the author

PAUL Wellings was born and raised in the ⌐   ` in the sixties, the eldest son of a PE teacher ⌐

After starting his journalistic caree⌐   , Paul landed a prestigious freelance job on ⌐   Musical Express, thanks to his best man To⌐   rst to write about the black R'n'B soul scen⌐   occer casual' movement.

In the early 1980s his group the ⌐   s released an LP, produced by the renowned reggae p.   Mad Professor (of Massive Attack fame), to rave reviews. .   up supported reggae legend Peter Tosh (Bob Marley's partner) on ⌐ ⌐.

He has also worked shifts on the showbiz pages of the *Daily Mirror* and London's *Evening Standard*.

As a sideline he was a two-step soul DJ with underground radio stations Laser and LWR (the station that launched Radio 1's Tim Westwood).

He has appeared on more than 20 TV shows discussing black music, youth culture, soccer casuals and pirate radio, and is featured in *S.O.U.L.*—the major ITV documentary about the history of black culture. He has written three books, *This is the Modern Word, East Ending* and *The Chaps,* plus the screenplay *Thieves.* He has also contributed to music magazines *Mojo* and *Echoes.*

In 1991 he moved into PR where he has a full-time career as well as being a freelance journalist for the *Sunday Mirror.*

He has been married to Lisa for 12 years and has two children.

I'M A JOURNALIST ... GET ME OUT OF HERE!

20 years' hacking through the media and music jungle

PAUL WELLINGS

The Progressive Press, Lancashire

First published 2004

The Progressive Press
3 June Avenue
Blackpool
Lancashire
FY4 4LQ

e-mail: barrymac@ukip.co.uk

Printed in Great Britain by Anthony Rowe Ltd, Chippenham, Wiltshire

Cover design by Mark Guest

British Library Cataloguing-in-Publication Data
A catalogue record for this book is available from the British Library

ISBN 0 9546121 1 6

CONTENTS

'In the old days men had the rack; now they have the press.'
Oscar Wilde, *The Soul of Man under Socialism*, 1891.

Introduction

VERY few jobs pay you great money to rub shoulders with such diverse characters as Michael Jackson, Reggie Kray and Julie Burchill. There are very few professions that will tell you to go on a world cruise to countries such as Bombay, Hong Kong, Egypt and Papua New Guinea and write about what you see. And there are even fewer roles that let you rant and rave about your opinions on sex, power, drugs, music and the arts. But the 'New Journalism', as the great Tom Wolfe called it, allows you to live out all those fantasies.

I first got the hold-the-front-page rush on joining the regional press before progressing to Fleet Street for the *Mirror* and *Evening Standard*. But I thought my dream job was going to be when I joined the *New Musical Express* covering black dance music and the soulhead dream, whose lifestyle was echoed by the Robert de Niro line from Scorsese's film *King of Comedy*: 'I'd rather be king for a day than schmuck for a lifetime.' Sadly it wasn't. The NME was a great start and I had the very best of times and the very worst of times there. Before I joined the NME I thought the music business was going to be an endless bout of sex, violence, drugs and funky music—but found out that was only on the first day.

Neil Spencer (now *The Observer*'s astrologer) was my editor at the NME, David Banks and Richard Stott (both great warriors against injustice) were my editors at the *Mirror* and the late great John Lees was my editor at the *Evening Standard*. Neil, David, Richard and John were all fabulous editors because they paid you on time and because they were loyal to their staff. Also huge thanks to Barry McLoughlin, my publisher and editor at the Progressive Press, for his belief in and development of the book—I am lucky to have these people on my side.

Big love and thanks go to the many people who urged me to write this book: Julie Burchill (the sharpest writer in the country), Spencer Bright (top biographer), Mick Mahoney (a real playwright for today), Peter York (always sartorially elegant and the cleverest man in Britain), and thanks to my former best man Tony Parsons for starting me off on this rocky road with the NME. No thanks to Blair!

As I look over my 20 years in journalism, it's like that rap song by Spooks where they say: 'You won't believe the things I've seen—far beyond your wildest dreams.' My reporting led me to receive death threats, to run with football hooligans, to get a gun put to my head while MC'ing in a pirate radio nightclub, to meet the meanest gangsters, to visit crackhouses, to see DJs relieve women backstage while playing records, to see gay sex live in a club and to see the most unlikely celebrities wasted on illegal substances. All human lowlife was there. It was like a Damon Runyon world of underworld characters with sobriquets such as Horace the Chiv and Jimmy the Bubble. As William Blake said, the road of excess leads to the palace of wisdom.

In all this I have learnt one vital lesson. Stay true to the things close to your heart and give a severe metaphoric kicking to the remainder. I look back at my irreverent, irresponsible, young self who had more chips on my shoulder than a tree surgeon and feel slightly embarrassed. In spite of that, I hope my column inches will leave you completely satisfied.

Paul Wellings
London 2004

PART ONE

1: Know your NME

TONY Blair was only an Ugly Rumour when he was reading the NME. Who could believe that the guitar-strumming university rock group star, who read the words of radical NME writers like Tony Parsons and Julie Burchill, could take us into five wars (count them) and widen the gap between rich and poor? But how did this happen and how did cheesygrin Prime Minister Blair come to control our media? I need to take you back to the years of Tory misrule and dive down some anecdotal alleyways.

It's a hot day in London's East End. I'm sitting in my home of Stepney, sipping an ice-cool lager outside the infamous Blind Beggar Pub in the Mile End Road. This is the drinking house where Ronnie Kray emptied a gun into a fellow villain and then joked he wanted a 'luger and lime'. Today it seems very tame.

Outside, the people bustle and hustle—the cockney tongue uniting them all: glamorous-gilded girls chatting about dating dos and don'ts with raucous dirty laughs; families struggling with shopping from Watney Market (Commercial Road, Stepney); rabbis; women in saris; and most noticeably cocky 'Chaps' (young wide-boys) shouting the odds with an exaggerated boxer's swagger, dressed in either downtown 'Homeboy' rap fan gear like fur-hooded black flight jackets and Kangol hats with an abundance of gold rings/bracelets, or smarter uptown Armani, Boss and Boy designer gear.

A beat box tape deck plays rough and tough rap music like Schooly D, LL Cool J, and Prince's Sign of The Times *line, 'They're high on crack, toting a machine gun', gets a rave reaction.*

Wild boys swap come-on looks with local 'fly girls' (soul fans) and dance away to the gangster boogie.

These chaps all grew up in London's docklands, born to wheel and deal. They are young hustlers—and 'little bits of business' is the name of their game.

Walking around this run-down manor—at the end of Wapping Wall—a dock wall has 'Yuppies Out', 'Burn Barratt', and 'Loot Asda' sprayed on it. Cynics say that Barratts build homes that no ordinary East Ender can afford; and Asda build hypermarkets on the area's last bit of green and pleasant land. This is the government's Enterprise Zone designated in 1981 to bring jobs and prosperity to the area.

The huge Millwall, India and London docks, once the 'pride of the Empire', are being transformed into yuppie housing schemes and office buildings, tempting companies with building subsidies and rate-free occupancy. To locals the Big Bang has been a damp fizzle. A third of local residents are out of work; new jobs are scarce and much of the housing is 'Council Hard To Let' with over half the people paying rent receiving housing benefit.

In a roughneck pub in Leman Street near the Police Station, the Chaps stand around a pool table. All dressed like French/Italian stylists with gelled-back cropped hair, Rayban shades, black Cecil Gee T-shirts and black 501s or trousers from Browns (South Molton Street). To gain respect in this area, pride in appearance is essential. They all grew up round here and their attitudes, like their parents', are nothing like TV's EastEnders—they're aggressive, working-class and conservative. Two-thirds of the club are white.

'EastEnders is a silly programme,' says gangly youth Paulie, a part-time DJ. 'You have all the blacks, Asians, whites, irons (gays), students and punks drinking in their local boozer getting on great and planning coach outings together. It's nothing like that.

'I ain't prejudiced or nothing—we do mix—we all like soul and rap music and go raving at clubs together—but usually you stay with one of your own. EastEnders is too miserable. We like having a wicked laugh and a wind-up round here. It keeps you alive.'

The Enterprise Zone run by the London Docklands Development Corporation (LDDC) also gets short shrift.

'The moneyed geezers are moving in and some local people are trying to buy their own places and council homes. But really the LDDC has done nothing for us. All the money is for Big Business. We get a few bob to keep us sweet. We don't want silly schemes like Action For Jobs at a "nifty" (£50) a week. We'd rather nick a container of leathers worth 10 grand,' says Neil.

Paulie, after a promising start boxing at Bethnal Green's Repton Club, began thieving at 15, the odd bike, joy-riding cars and hoisting shops for records and clothes to fence. He used to be part of West Ham FC's notorious ICF—Inter-City Firm of hooligans—but he has 'progressed' from that now.

He says: 'When there's no decent jobs about, you're forced into doing things a bit illegal. I used to fly-pitch moody (fake) gold earrings down Petticoat Lane with my mate; cane rich outsiders' motors for car stereos and sell them to a local cab firm. That's a regular touch—the Robin Hood thing—"taxing" from the rich to help the poor people. This is our area, it'll never not be our area. The real crooks round here are the men in grey suits who get LDDC money, yet somehow that's kosher.'

Persistent crimes have led to frequent stop-and-search police procedures. Distrust between the police and the Chaps is high, especially as the police concentrate on protecting the property of newer, richer inhabitants who've been harassed and had homes fire-bombed.

Although the Chaps call their area a 'Khazi', don't make a big point about being East Enders and dream of moving to Essex suburbia—to outsiders they are violently territorial and loyal to this dilapidated part of East London.

Paulie says: 'I can see it getting worse. Yuppies' cars and property will get vandalised, they'll be scared to move here. There'll be a lot more hatred, a lot of people doing bird for their area.'

Some of Paulie's family live in the area, some have escaped to Essex and the Norfolk seaside resorts. He left home to live his own life. There are about 50 empty flats on his family's old estate. The council seems reluctant to fill them and housing associations can't help them. He lives with his best friend in a small one-bedroom flat.

'I reckon the council wants to get rid of the locals,' he says. 'All these toffee-nosed gits who've paid a quarter of a million pounds for their penthouses don't want rough and ready cockneys like me walking down their road.'

What worries Chaps like Neil is kids 'chasing the dragon' rather than chasing dreams.

'If you're one of the Chaps, you pride yourself on thinking on your feet, living on your wits. That "you make a pound note—I make a pound note" attitude. But kids getting bored are knocking out and doing drugs on the estates like speed, puff and smack. And they lose all ambition for jobs, cars and a decent home. They give up. I smoke the odd spliff now and again and love a booze. But really drugs is for mugs. To survive you've got to keep a clear head.'

All this is a million miles away from the EastEnders soap world idolised by Style mag The Face. The Mean Streets of Walford - what a joke that is. The Face's self-appointed youth spokesman Robert Elms ought to pay a visit to East London—to Dalston's Sangriham Road 'Homeboy Front Line'—where depending on your preference you can buy an ounce of drawer (cannabis) or a Magnum 44 gun. It's a bit like the Hole In The Wall Club - guns must be worn. Dangerous Times indeed.

Whereas amusing TV chaps like Arthur Daley and villains in the unauthentic film Empire State are said in some out-of-touch quarters to be 'too near the mark', it is clear they would not last five minutes with the real East End chaps. Who are they trying to kid?

That was a pre-Blair story, when a lot of ordinary people dreamed of a Labour government, which I wrote for the *Evening Standard*. It was meant to be objective, impartial journalism. In fact, it was the story of people I knew in my life. Admittedly I was more enlightened than some of the street urchins I went around with—but it was my life. A blagger's life—liberating tens of thousands of pounds-worth of CDs, videos and books from multi-national companies for review purposes. But as an intelligent socialist (isn't an unintelligent socialist an oxymoron?) I had a crystal-clear conscience about this as it demonstrated redistributive wealth. When I talk about being a blagger I am, of course, not referring to the criminal argot for armed robber (in the John McVicar, public enemy No. 1 mode) but just high-spirited mischief. I would charm my way into celebrity parties, backstage events, film premieres—with more front than Margate.

In fact, I bluffed my way into journalism and am still bluffing in the PR world (as a poacher turned gamekeeper, defecting to the other side). If the truth were told, most journalists are bluffers to some degree. I rather like the self-deprecating working title used by Britain's most trenchant and abrasive columnist, Julie Burchill, for her autobiography *Now wash your hands*—because us old hacks are naughty by nature and we rarely take ourselves too seriously. After all I was not the new Will 'Brain the size of a planet' Self, just someone with a minor talent for writing which had been exhausted a long time ago. To misquote *Monty Python* I was a lucky, lucky bastard who had met the right people at the right place at the right time. But I was tenacious and thick-skinned, which were essential journalistic qualities.

In 2002, using my NUJ card, I talked my way backstage (past three security gates) at a Sex Pistols concert in Crystal Palace ('Pistols at the Palace' mock Jubilee event) only to be stopped at the final gate and told I didn't have a backstage pass. But persistence overcomes resistance and I suddenly spotted Pistols guitarist Steve Jones going to the Portaloo outside and shouted: 'Steve, I'm press—any chance of meeting Johnny?' He waved me past security guards (much to their chagrin) and said: 'He's all right—he's with us!' Thanking him, I made my way inside to where Pistols front man John Lydon was holding court. In February 2004 Lydon was to stun his fans by agreeing to take part in the prime-time ITV reality show *I'm a Celebrity ... Get Me Out of Here!* He was pursued into the Australian jungle by cries of 'sell-out', but his premature departure, accompanied by a valedictory volley of four-letter expletives, reassured a generation of old punks that his wealthy LA lifestyle had not mellowed him too dramatically. As Tony Parsons put it in his *Mirror* column, 'John

Lydon didn't quit the show ... because he thought he was going to lose. He walked away because he thought he was going to win.'

Backstage at Crystal Palace in 2002, I chatted away with Lydon for half an hour and he was angry about a lot of things, particularly Tony Blair when he said with venom: 'Never, trust a toff—never, ever, ever.' Much like the sleeve notes for the programme for the concert where he said: 'The ruling classes have let this country down, they should be ashamed of themselves, but we haven't. We swore we would never re-form, but we did, but that's because there's a reason for it, and it's not about money, it's a celebration. This is our Jubilee. It's us or fake middle class values ... People look to Britain for ideas, it's a fact—Blair, the monarchy, the way we run the country, it's killing that off.'

He discussed lame-brain racist punks who had thrown missiles at the reggae sound system warming up for the Pistols, which led to him coming on stage during their set, bowing to the reggae DJ as they played Beenie Man's 'Who Am I?' in a 'we are not worthy' gesture. He discussed his ridiculous Little Englander taunt 'Keep the Pound'. He also discussed whether John Wayne was a right-wing bigot and the merits of the phrase 'never apologise and explain' and he simply said 'the Duke was an OK guy'. I then got invited as Johnny's new best friend to a private party at an as-yet unopened club in south-west London listening to Mr Lydon's favourite Trance DJ—staying with the legendary punk singer until 5am with the usual pills, thrills and bellyaches going round. After asking him what made him proud to be British, he said with his usual acid wit, 'Living in LA!'

I came home on the milk train at 7am and my long-suffering wife said: 'Where the hell have you been?' I replied: 'You're not going to believe this, but I got involved with Johnny Rotten all night.' She eventually forgave me. A leading trade magazine picked up on the story, saying: 'Those members of the public relations world who started life as journalists (traitors, but better-paid traitors) still manage to find their former skills coming in handy, using their aged press cards to help blag themselves into some pretty odd situations. Media man Paul Wellings used his press card to get backstage to meet the Sex Pistols at a gig in South London this summer. Quite what was discussed at the after-show party until the very early hours of the morning is still a bit hazy, but we feel safe in suggesting that a publicity campaign for Paul's company fronted by Johnny Rotten is a very, very remote possibility.'

The NME's veteran Steven Wells summed up the day at Crystal Place Sports Centre perfectly: 'The Sex Pistols were the last band to mean something to everyone. They were the folk devils who changed everything—art, politics, fashion, music—*everything*.

'John Lydon—a curious cross between Victor Meldrew and an es-presso-overdosed ferret—roundly curses the Queen Mum and Tony Blair... It is ugly and beautiful and witty and stupid and bitter and twisted. And magnificently, tragically English. Pig-ignorant genius—it's all that really stops us just being Americans with bad teeth. Face it—these dead-donkey flogging, money-grabbing fat fuckers are us. The best of us and the worst of us. The Sex Pistols are the living heart and soul of a nation of drunken barbarian scum. We might as well be proud of them.'

Tony Parsons in the NME once described Lydon as 'the well-mannered boy spastic-dancing and looking like a week-old corpse still shaking with the shock of the red-hot piece of wire that a sadistic under-taker shoved up his anal passage at the very instant of death.' While his partner in grime Julie Burchill sneered when sitting at the feet of the 17-year-old Lydon: 'Go away—you're too old.'

But the NME was his biggest champion in the early days: 'The heaviest artillery in the Pistols' arsenal was that they had Johnny Rotten. For over twenty years rock music had been a metaphor for sex, drugs and violence. But it had always been hinted at, never confronted directly. Rotten destroyed the pose and replaced it with his own version of reality, and it was the most mesmerising spectacle that ever hunched its way on to a stage.'

The journalistic upstart had met the spectacle. My journalism was 'from the inside looking out' rather than the traditional 'from the outside looking in'. It was literature in a hurry. The semi-autobiographical pieces I wrote, with the names changed to protect the innocent, completely con-tradicted Blair's view that 'we're all middle class now'.

But how did this unorthodox approach to journalism start and where does Blair fit into all this? Let me introduce you to someone in the media who was one of New Labour's biggest fans.

2: Writers and writing

TONY Parsons was gorgeous. Not in a homoerotic way, but his writing was gorgeous and his attitude was gorgeous. And from 1983-95 I loved him like a brother. I was to fall out of love with him—but more about that later. In my eyes Tony was one of the best, most feisty prole pop writers after Julie Burchill and Danny Baker. I interviewed him while I was working for the rockist weekly *Sounds* (under the dreadful soulboy moniker Jimmy Mack) and my life would never be the same again. He taught me that journalism was an honourable, noble profession and gave me the break I needed.

'Father, son, husband, partner, lover, lad, breadwinner, domestic technician, macho boy, sensitive soul,' said Simon Hattenstone in *The Guardian*. Tony Parsons, punk journalist turned media big mouth turned novelist, has been the lot. In Parsons' case a massive mouth (literally). All mouth and Paul Smith trousers. His failed attempt at a TV chatshow was actually called *Big Mouth*. Parsons was never a good front man, but a master of the acerbic soundbite.

Parsons is the establishment's token prole. He wears his working-class hero badge to his chest, never changing his accent, saying 'fanks' and 'fings' despite spending his adult life doing the media rounds. He was used on BBC2's cultural TV show *Late Review,* until he fell out with the producer because, unlike any of the other guests, he was not prepared to work once a month—it was every week or nothing for our Tone.

'He's not a person—he's a journalist,' said a character in Cameron Crowe's *Almost Famous*, his authentic, autobiographical film about seventies rock journalism. Just like the lead character in that movie, as a pop journalist you feel constantly like the enemy—'because you write what you see'. The only fault of the film was the deification of rock scribe Lester Bangs who in my humble opinion was hopelessly overrated and like many of us just got lucky. About the only thing he wrote that I liked was in 1969 when he sent a caustic review of the MC5's 'Kick Out the Jams' to *Rolling Stone* magazine, with a covering letter that read: 'Look, fuckheads, I'm as good a writer as any you've got in there. You'd better print this or give me the reason why.' They did and for the next 13 years, until he died from an overdose of painkillers aged 33, Bangs hung out with rock stars, got high and got laid and wrote about music for *Rolling Stone*, *Creem*, and the *Village Voice*.

Like Bangs I've certainly been very lucky; I make a living from the only thing I like and about the only thing I can do. James Cameron once said that being a journalist allows you to 'swim in every ocean and make love in every continent' and I wanted to just dive in. But also, just like *Vanity Fair*'s Christopher Hitchens, I would sit at my typewriter every day and fear 'today is the day they are going to find me out.' I was a cynical hack and literary pickpocket who liberated words from the best. In journalism, if we're honest, everyone steals a little. Complete originality is rare. Shakespeare acknowledged in sonnet 76: 'So all my best is dressing old words new/Spending again, what is already spent.' I was one of those who represented the unacceptable face of popular journalism. I was to reporting what lockjaw was to conversation. Many an accurate word is spoken in jest: as Sinatra said, 'a journalist is someone who lies in the sun all day and then goes home to his typewriter to lie some more'. But as Julie Burchill puts it in *Sex and Sensibility,* 'Whenever I read writers on writing, I'm proud to call myself a hack. The vices of journalism are plain to see and endlessly itemised, but its virtues—self-deprecation, graft, lack of phoney baloney—are rarely mentioned.'

I was never star-struck with celebrity and instead would prefer the company of roughneck urchin chums rather than showbiz parties. I always found the majority of celebrities were over-pampered *prima donnas*. Recently I saw one of my heroes Billy Connolly on a TV documentary when he spoke about the artist David Hockney. 'I'm lucky enough to be his next-door neighbour actually—I hope it doesn't sound like name-dropping,' followed by: 'He's a genius. A personal friend of mine you know. Us geniuses all hang out together in the geniuses club.' Billy, you've joined the luvvie club, my friend, hanging out with Prince Charles, and need to check your ego in at reception. Once I berated Ben Elton (another member of the writers' luvvie club) in London's Dean Street for ten minutes (much to the amusement of passers-by) about working with Lloyd-Webber and playing the Queen's Golden Jubilee and betraying everything he stood for with a new brand of Bollinger Bolshevism. (Melvyn Bragg similarly felt the rough edge of my tongue in public.) But in all fairness to Mr Elton he did say he was 'left of Labour and not a Blairite'—so he redeemed himself slightly in my eyes. Frankly, though, as I'm so opinionated, it's a mystery why I've not been banned from polite society altogether. I can only assume that when dealing with people like me, the media establishment (I have had furious rows on prime time TV with broadcasting fat cats like Alan Yentob and David Elstein) shares the view expressed so colourfully by the late US President Lyndon Johnson: 'It's better to have him inside the tent pissing out than outside the tent pissing in.'

Back to the writers. Prior to Parsons I had been writing about rock-jawed heroes in books for school chums that were passed around avidly. I lived in a land of make-believe when I was a kid. I was always telling very elaborate lies and making up stories. That led directly to writing. I always loved writing at school. As my only strong subject at school was English, I was indentured to go to the Harlow Centre of Journalism (where *Mirror* Editor Piers Morgan and Dire Straits' Mark Knopfler went—I hate name-droppers, as I said to Nelson Mandela last week), by Home Counties Newspapers. I then went on to write about cats up trees and the Great Train Robbery revisited for a local paper (where my Evelyn Waugh-style 'scoop' was tracking down a Nazi living in Leighton Buzzard and getting him to dress up in his regalia for a front-page splash). All the hack chat was of the 'stone' (composing room), 'body-type' (the main typeface in which an article is set), 'screamers' (exclamation marks) and 'splashes' (front-page exclusives).

I started my journalistic career on the *Beds & Bucks Observer* entrusted with the task of rewriting the Townswomen's Guild and Women's Institute reports! I never knew longer days—except for my work as the union father of the chapel (chairman of the union branch)—where I fought for truth, justice and the British way. But now with an entry into the pop press, I thought I was about to enter a world of sex and debauchery and get paid for it. After all, journalists are lying, cheating, cocaine-sniffing scum—what better company could I ask for? Yet my pop life was actually not short enough for my liking, even though I was let out on parole after four years for being on my worst behaviour. When Nick Hornby said in *High Fidelity* that working on the NME was the best job in the world, he wasn't talking about the early 1980s.

Compared with most of the middle-aged, middle-class men in leather jackets who toil for a laughably small return for the music press, I was a complete and utter *arriviste*. The *Sounds* editor Eric Fuller (who was jokingly referred to as 'Fullershit' in the paper), despite sharing my love of Ska/Reggae, didn't feature me in his future plans. Garry Bushell, then a good socialist (who was offered a Labour candidacy in a safe Welsh seat) rather than the reactionary figure he has become, gave me as much work as he could. Garry wrote beautifully, wittily and passionately about the mighty two-tone movement—which I thought was more revolutionary than punk. In the light of this I decided to make my own future and promptly met Tony Parsons, with a view to getting on the NME.

3: The best job in the world

WON over by my magnetic personality (it says here), Parsons took me to his macho bosom and introduced me to the NME's editor Neil Spencer and I got the gig. It seems ridiculous now, but in the period between 1974 and 1984 the NME was a Godsend—the epitome of Cool—for people like me growing up in the London new towns. I used to love the iconoclastic cartoons of Ray Lowry and the way on the Teasers letters page Danny Baker and Monty Smith would just answer someone's verbose rambling attack with the phrase: 'You're an idiot, mate!'

In 2002 the NME celebrated its 50th birthday. Launched in 1952 by Maurice Kinn, it is credited with reviving Frank Sinatra's career with one of its articles—'a pint-size genius, a performer loaded with charisma who could take a song and reveal a world of loss, love, turmoil and anguish'—and also championed the early work of The Beatles and the Rolling Stones. 'The Stones are way out. You could feel the Empire Pool shaking to its foundations.' It embraced punk: 'The Sex Pistols play loud, clean and tight and they don't mess around. Watching them gives that same clenched-gut feeling that you get when you see the lads hanging out on the corner looking for some action and you wonder if that action might be you.' It celebrated The Smiths and New Order in the 1980s and then supported the Madchester acid house scene and Britpop bands such as Oasis in the nineties: 'Oasis were magical. The world would be a darker place without them.' The new bands they pioneered lately would be Lost Prophets, 'Six young lads from the Welsh Valleys—package them right and they will be bloody huge'; The Music, 'Four young misfits from Leeds who are powerful heavy psychedelia comparable to The Verve'; Electric Soft Parade, 'They are a couple of posh kids from Brighton but they may just have saved British pop music'; and The Coral, 'The most extraordinary band that Liverpool and the UK has produced for years. In the flesh they are from another planet.'

But perhaps the biggest interest the NME attracted from mainstream broadcast and print media was when it ran a cover story accusing Tony Blair of being a sell-out, with every rock star available saying his Cool Britannia had turned into Cruel Britannia. Radical writer Danny Hammill said Blair had conducted a ruthless crusade in his determination to forge a New 'Cool' Britain. This 'revolution' from above had been planned, conducted and engineered by a veritable army of spin doctors, PR consultants, advertising and media contacts. Inspired by Bill Clinton and the vapid razzmatazz that is official politics, no gimmick or PR opportunity was missed—nothing too shameful or embarrassing.

It is fair to say that New Labour is obsessed by the power of image and by the art of marketing. Tony Blair and his team have sought to wrap themselves with an aura of youthful vibrancy—a cosmetic distancing from the old fogey-ist culture of 'the Establishment'. For the Blairites it was essential for New Labour to tap into and misappropriate youth culture—and popular culture in general. One fertile territory, naturally, was pop music. The rising stars and heroes of Britpop had to be schmoozed. (Many of the young Blairites instinctively feel, no doubt including The Great Control Freak himself, more at home with popular culture than the bourgeois-dominated high culture of opera, classical music, ballet etc.)

This does not make Blair especially unique. The Harold Wilson government similarly attempted to connect with the mop-topped optimism of the Beatles and their devoted followers. High-profile publicity shots of Wilson joking with members of the Fab Four sent out the message that we were witnessing a rebirth of Labour—the 'white heat' of technology aligned with the semi-hysteria of Beatlemania. Britain was back on the map—*and it was cool this time*. Kinnock tried the same with the Tracey Ullman video and the whole Red Wedge experiment.

The rise of bands like Oasis, Pulp, Blur, Radiohead, The Verve and Prodigy has also been seen as the dawn of a new Britain. Noel Gallagher of Oasis, an unashamed and open 'druggie', visited No. 10. The Catholic church-attending Tony Blair warmly embraced Gallagher. Like virtually all the Britpoppers, Gallagher treated Blair as a conquering hero, a righteous knight who had slain the dreaded Tory beast. Blair seemed on the buzz. Gallagher said at an award ceremony in 1997 'power to the people—Tony Blair's the man.' It was no accident that Blair did not invite members of Pink Floyd, Jethro Tull or Yes to his post-victory jamborees. Gallagher would later disown Blair, saying: 'Whenever there is a conservative, Bible-waving half-wit ruling in the White House—whether it's Bush, his father or Reagan—there is war. Whoever is the British Prime Minister is tied to America. It's been that way since the Second World War, and even Tony Blair can't change that.

'Politics is like football for me. Labour is my team and even if you don't like a striker, you don't give up supporting the whole team,' he said. 'Labour is the lesser of two evils. What else should we have? Anarchy? Someone has to be responsible.'

Everything seemed to be going Blair's way. Stories appeared in the music press about Blair's guitar-playing activities. Mat Snow, my former reviews editor on the NME and former editor of the 'fortysomething' music magazine *Mojo*, recounted his days with Blair in the Ugly Rumours. Blair as sub-Keith Richards. Thanks to the Britpoppers, New Labour was linked with success 'by simply co-opting the most superficial elements of a notional Cool Britannia,' as Sean O'Hagan wrote in *The Guardian*.

But things had started to go horribly wrong. Cracks were appearing in the crumbling Cool Britannia monolith. First it was John Prescott, a living symbol of uncool Britannia (except for throwing a right-hander at a bigoted fuel protester). At a Britpop award ceremony, he had a bucket of water thrown over him by Danbert Nobacon of the anarchist band, Chumbawamba. Nobacon's act of liquid terrorism was on behalf of 'single mothers, pensioners, sacked dockworkers, people being forced into workfare, people who will be denied legal aid, students who will be denied the free university education that the entire front bench benefited from, the homeless and all the underclasses who are now suffering at the hands of the Labour government.'

Then we had the vicious—and articulate—attack on Blair by *New Musical Express*. For good or bad, NME remains an influential weathervane of pop-cultural taste. Its core readership is young, predominantly white, male and urban. To alienate this constituency could spell disaster for New Labour. This NME assault must have dealt a hammer blow to the Tony Blair image department—and to the whole Cool Britannia project. Martin Jacques got it right when he described the NME editorial as 'the most important political event this week' (*The Observer*).

The NME front page was pasted with the headline, 'Ever had the feeling you've been cheated?', alongside a large picture of a distinctly mean and nasty-looking Tony Blair. The contents reflected the cover. The editorial, entitled 'The Labour government's war on you', condemned the whole gamut of New Labour's initiatives: welfare to work, tuition fees, curfews and the war on drugs. The approach of New Labour to drugs, for instance, is denounced as the living negation of 'coolness'.

As *NME* says: '*Our* music, *our* culture, *our* collective sweat of our groovy brows has been bundled up and neatly repackaged and given a cute little brand name and is being used by New Labour spin doctors to give this hideously reactionary New Labour government a cachet of radical credibility. A credibility of which it is utterly undeserving.'

In the light of Prescott's watery ordeal, the NME concludes with a warning: 'But New Labour might be better advised to treat the soaking as a warning from us all. As a warning that New Labour's honeymoon is over. That rock music's decades-old, instinctive and deep-seated pro-Labour sympathies have, in the past nine months, been chipped away to almost nothing. Good morning, Mr Blair, this is your wake-up call.'

Blair's former supporters turned into opponents. In *NME* we read about Alan McGee of Oasis record company Creation and former general New Labour consultant. He headed the Music Industry Task Force and donated £50,000 to New Labour's election campaign. McGee was appalled by New Labour's welfare-to-work schemes, whereby musicians—he singles them out—have to take *any* employment offered. 'Labour is making it worse for musicians,' McGee points out: 'I was on an Enterprise Allowance Scheme for a year after I worked on British Rail and that's how I got Creation together in 1983. If I had been forced to take a job then I would probably still be at British Rail now.' It was a powerful, coherent critique of New Labour attacking Welfare to Work, student fees, the continued criminalisation of cannabis and curfews for under-18s.

According to NME, New Labour's general attack on benefits threatens to wipe-out the next generation of artists. The dole was a primitive form of arts subsidy. Without it, it would have been impossible for artists to emerge and nurture their talent—which takes *time*. It is no accident that the new wave of Britpop emerged at the time it did—after years of mass unemployment under the Tories. In a statement to the NME, The Verve echoed the point: 'Of course we were on the dole when we left college. We needed just enough money to live on whilst we got it together. We wrote a lot of the first album during that time. You need time and space to grow as a band or, come to think of it, in any art form.'

The response from its 600,000 readers was phenomenal. 'What really pisses them off is the feeling they're being sold down the river to the concerns of Middle England,' said deputy editor at the time John Mulvey. One of the many letters NME published said: 'Listen up, Tony, us teenagers aren't all shit-for-brains, alcopops-fixated, apolitical no-hopers who can't think for themselves or form their own opinions.'

Mulvey was 'incredibly heartened' by the support for the NME's political stance. 'I thought the young were less political and more apathetic. Maybe, just maybe, there is some kind of political resistance going on.'

Gordon Brown's budget speech at this time intensified the philistine, anti-working class measures inaugurated by the Tories—and now being perfected by New Labour. Brown intended to drive working class youth into jobs by bribing the bosses to take on the long-term unemployed. As *The Guardian* semi-approvingly put it, 'Work has acquired ideological status ... New Labour is all about encouraging aspiration, however lowly, rather than cushioning under-privilege, however chronic.' It concluded that Blair and Brown have 'the faith that people can be made to want to work'. Farewell to art and culture from below—if they get their way.

Splits from above were expected: the Countryside Alliance march and Diana's funeral demonstrated that. But splits emerging in Cool Britannia were particularly damaging for New Labour. While Britpop musicians may not be humble now, most of them are from humble origins.

These bands, through their music and the very fact of success, exert influence; the songs have resonance among working class youth. Their became informed by a spirit of strident anti-Blairism ... leading to them joining the *Mirror*'s anti-war campaign. But more about that in the second half. The NME was never to back a Blair initiative again.

The NME reported that Blur's lead singer, Damon Albarn, was one of the most outspoken opponents of the war against Iraq, which was even more remarkable given his close connection to New Labour just eight years earlier. By 1998 Albarn had already been leading the charge against New Labour's plans to scrap student grants. After the government introduced the New Deal scheme, Alan McGee told the press that Labour was proving to be worse than the Tories. During the London mayoral elections Albarn publicly came out in support of Ken Livingstone—the anti-Blair ticket at the time (despite cuddly Ken getting invited back into the fold now).

The divorce was complete when Blair backed Bush's war in Iraq. Albarn, Massive Attack and Coldplay all came out against the war. After years of silence, the godfather of Britpop, Paul Weller, played at a Stop the War Coalition benefit concert in London. The NME gave significant coverage to anti-government stories. One of the latest pop stars to condemn Blair in the NME is Ms Dynamite who says: 'In terms of gun violence and gun crime it's obvious—the problem is poverty. The government have to give young people education and jobs, then none of this would be occurring.'

The star also criticised the then Culture Minister, Kim Howells, for comments about rap music and gun violence. She said: 'People can make out they are interested in a problem, but then they go and make comments like they have about our music. It shows no one's listening, no one's understanding and no one cares.' In September 2003 rapper Dizzee Rascal won the coveted Mercury music prize and the media picked up on the line from his uncompromising album *Boy In Da Corner*, 'I'm a problem for Anthony Blair', asking how can a boy who went through our so-called Welfare State be so angry?

As Martin Clark from *Mixmag*, writing for *The Guardian*, explains, 'There is precious little dialogue between the establishment and the street. Locked into US hip-hop, Jamaican ragga and UK garage culture, Dizzee and his peers couldn't be more isolated from Westminster.'

In its attempt to be 'down with the kids' in a fantastic 50-year souvenir tribute edition, the NME produced the most pale, male and stale top 50 influential music acts list I've ever seen. The Smiths were bizarrely at number 1 (as another journalist said to me, the only band they've ever influenced were Gene) and Bob Dylan at 38? But the biggest error was there was only one black artist—Bob Marley, in halfway down—and virtually no women. It failed to give a mention to such influential pop giants as Jimi Hendrix, Marvin Gaye, James Brown, Stevie Wonder, Aretha Franklin, Lauryn Hill, Macy Gray, Missy Elliott, Billie Holiday and Prince.

Recent editor Ben Knowles in the tribute issue says: 'It's been an opportunity to reread some of the finest rock journalism the world has ever seen and to rediscover the most iconic photo-archive in the world.' It may been 50 years of sex, drugs and rock'n'roll but as Johnny Rotten said, 'I use the NME, I use anarchy.' Lots of people used the NME. Under the editorship of Neil Spencer, it started off as all Weller and The Jam, and the new breed of writers split their time between pretending to be bohemian or the intellectual funk boys. John Lydon accurately describes NME writers as 'the kind of lonely kids who were bullied at school and here was their big vendetta'. Julie Burchill had different memories of the most memorable NME she ever worked on. 'Sorry, but I don't remember anything! Just say that.'

Recently in *The Independent*, the veteran former NME hack Charles Shaar Murray was lauding the 'more innocent' era of the sixties and early seventies and attacking the current charts. I tend to agree with the view of *The Guardian*'s excellent pop writer Alexis Petridis that pop looks good. When I look around the CDs in my local megastore, I don't see the death rattle of a once-great culture (despite Blair's sanitising influence) but fantastically exciting stuff such as The Streets' intelligent slant on garage and truly innovative material by Aaliyah, Missy Elliott and Erykah Badu. Black music to me just gets stronger and stronger. Shaar Murray goes on to claim that we need to compare 2002 with the golden ages of 1967 or 1977, asserting the 'best stuff is on the independent fringes'. This is cack. In 1967 Englebert Humperdink, Harry Secombe, Cliff Richard and Vince Hill were outselling everybody. In 1977 the biggest sellers were David Soul, Boney M and Manhattan Transfer. Admittedly the best stuff has always been on the fringes—but it's got more chance to cross over nowadays. Who'd have believed a tune like Afroman's dope anthem 'I Got High' would have hit the number one spot and got unlimited airplay in 1977? Gareth Gates is just the new Vince Hill. Homer Simpson once announced 'everyone knows rock attained perfection in 1974' and Shaar Murray is in danger of becoming another ageing rock critic (like me) harping on about a golden age. I'm determined not to turn into my dad and watch *Top of the Pops* and scream 'Turn this rubbish down!'

Pop music today is not dead—it's just starting to smell a bit. Old NME critics are not going to ever kill it off. And old rock journalists don't die—they just go on trips.

The NME outlasted other magazines such as *Sounds, Record Mirror* and *Select* and then merged with long-time rival *Melody Maker*, founded in 1926 and now has a new(ish) editor, Conor McNicholas. But despite recently being overtaken by metal maestros *Kerrang!* as the best-selling music magazine, former editor Ben Knowles insists the NME will remain 'the history of rock 'n' roll'. He said: 'This year, we will have ten new acts on the cover that will still be there in five years' time. The British rock scene will continue growing.' But as an old person's young person, I have to admit—at risk of a terrible review—I've never seen the NME look so dumbed-down as it is now. In my view the only decent writers they have currently are old-timers like Dele Fadele and Steven Wells. And they wouldn't get on a list of the all time greats: Nick Kent, Charles Shaar Murray, Julie Burchill, Tony Parsons, Ian Penman, Danny Baker (even though he claims he based most of his writings on the 'Best of SJ Perelman' books) and Paolo Hewitt. Not forgetting the 'star' journalists who passed through: Chrissie Hynde (Pretenders) and Neil Tennant (Pet Shop Boys).

As myth has it, around 1978 the editor of the *New Musical Express* walked into the office and decreed that it was now a punk magazine. Anyone who did not want to work for a punk magazine could go forth and multiply. And talking to *The Guardian*'s Ciar Byrne, one year after being appointed editor of the NME, Conor McNicholas was planning his own radical revolution. NME the weekly music newspaper is dead; long live NME the magazine.

He says: 'I decided there was no point in running it like a newspaper any more. Most of the kids who are reading NME now don't even know that *Melody Maker* ever existed.' His target audience is 19 years old.

'The great thing about being a 50-year-old magazine is that you've got this fantastic longevity and brand awareness; but with anything that's 50 you tend to get a lot of dust knocking around the corners,' admits McNicholas.

'Previously I think the NME has been quite an arrogant product. It has been quite difficult to get into—it was almost a badge of honour once you had made your way into a world where there were lots of in-jokes and lots of references that were never explained. What I want to do is to make sure that we retain all of our authority, all of the things that make NME great, but just make the club a hell of a lot easier to join.

'The music scene was shifting, but the music scene wouldn't look the way it does at the moment if it wasn't for the way the NME has played it. All the bands that are knocking about that are exciting now—the Strokes, the White Stripes, Interpol, Polyphonic Spree, Yeah Yeah Yeahs—we wrote about all of them first.

'There's some brilliant pop music around, some amazing rap, hip-hop, I wanted to make sure we weren't seen as a white boy guitar rag, because it isn't like that. It's got to embrace everything.'

He is also keen to appeal equally to women, admitting that in the past the NME has been seen as a 'bit of a boys' club'. 'It's all very well to produce something that has got this fantastic 50-year-old legacy. NME, when it has been at its best, has ignored that legacy completely and just ploughed forward talking to the music fan of the day. When you edit looking over your shoulder at the past, that's when you start getting into difficulty. There are no rules, and God knows people have shaken up the NME a hundred times since it started.'

I started reading the *New Musical Express* when it gave away a free *Monty Python* flexi-disc in 1974 and stayed with it until I started working for the magazine in 1984.

From the late seventies writers like Burchill and Parsons seemed as though they were writing the diary of my life. Their book *The Boy Looked At Johnny* to me was the best book on the music business I'd ever read and, despite what everyone else says nowadays, got it spectacularly RIGHT. There was never a better pop exposé before or since. I remember buying it at an alternative bookshop called Book Marks in London in 1978 and saw it as an act of insurrection. On the back of the book Burchill and Parsons, looking like the youngest, coolest people you'd ever seen, called themselves the 'only unbiased rock writers in the world'—'no trips to America, no free lunches, no payola, no nothing'. It went on to say: 'Brought to the notorious NME from school and night shifts to shake up one of the youngest, wealthiest and most self-inflated industries of the twentieth century, they have been threatened with everything from three-piece, legal suited lawyers to tooled-up Lower East Side gangsters. Read by two million readers every week and reviled by the cocaine-scum rock stars and the Valium-choking record conglomerates, they wrote *The Boy Looked At Johnny*, not as a book for those who seek to keep their idols cocooned in soft-focus press officer mythology, but as a book that blows the lid off rock and roll for the first and last time. Handle with caution; the authors come not to praise rock but to bury it.' Pete Townsend of The Who on seeing it called it 'gross callousness'. Radio One DJ John Peel, writing for *Sounds,* said: 'Disconcerting, uncompromising. I have over the years, heard so many musicians say what they would do when they achieved a position of influence only to see them do the opposite that I should be disillusioned totally. But I'm not and that is why I carry on doing what I do—and I hope that Tony Parsons and Julie Burchill, despite their assertion that rock is dead, will likewise continue, even though it is on a rival newspaper.'

Subtitled 'the obituary of rock and roll' it started with the lyrics of Julie Burchill's favourite album, Patti Smith's *Horses,* which she reviewed on school notebook paper handwritten to get the NME job. 'The boy looked at Johnny. Johnny wanted to run. But the movie kept moving as planned' (Copyright Linda Music, 1975). The cover had a rebellious Johnny Rotten giving the reverse Winston Churchill sign coming out of court. With love to 'everyone else on the same side at Lewisham, 1977 and especially for our parents'. The book's heroes were Tom Robinson—'You, you will be king'—and PolyStyrene—'And you will be Queen'. The book started with the immortal opener 'Bob Dylan, broke his neck—close but no cigar' and ended with the words 'It's only rock and roll and it's plastic, plastic, yes it is.' Probably the only line that's dated in it was 'Compared to the Tom Robinson Band, every other rock musician is wanking into the wind'. But in the spring of 1978 in Carnaby Street that statement was probably justified. Having said that I'd crawl over a million bland Travis and Coldplay albums to get to the TRB's *Power In The Darkness* LP or even *Chas 'n' Dave's Greatest Hits* come to that.

4: Childhood idylls and pop idols

NOSTALGIA ain't what is used to be but when you hit 40 you realise there's nothing more embarrassing than an old duffer like me trying to be cool. The older you get, the more you notice age. That's something I've come to realise these past couple of years. It seems ridiculous to me that I can easily recollect both George Best and Muhammad Ali in their prime. Somehow, that just doesn't seem right. Surely these guys shouldn't age.

Nor I, for that matter. I remember black-and-white TV and *Star Trek* when it first came out. I remember watching *Top of the Pops* and thinking it was just 'the best'. I remember eight-track stereo cassette and thinking just how state-of-the-art we all thought they were. As a kid I used to adore toy money, Corgi and Dinky toy cars (at ten shillings a time) and fake cigarettes. *Dandy* and *Beano* comics were heaven-sent in my youthful eyes as was Cream Soda pop and Linda Thorsen from *The Avengers*. I was also heavily into silver identity bracelets. What's more, hearing the ice cream van was every bit as good as getting a hard-on in my early teens, which regularly seemed to happen for hardly any reason at all back then. Does anyone remember Marnalito in the *High Chaperal*? I wanted to look like him or Kung Fu king Bruce Lee! And what about those little orange vinyl records you used to have to play at 78rpm rather than 45 or 33—does anyone remember those? Then there was the 1970 World Cup song 'Back Home' and collecting all those World Cup cards (from the newsagents) and coins (from Esso) and phew ... just how hot was it that summer in '76?

Yet if you asked me today to tell what I think is the happiest moment of my life to date, I truly think it was when John Barnes got the best England goal ever, seemingly running the whole length of the field, and defying all the race-haters in an international friendly. The best moments of my life have always been at R'n'B clubs DJ'ing, at Notting Hill Carnival or at football. But if you'd asked me back in 1972, I'd have probably said getting my staid, fully mudguarded three-speed bicycle transformed into the equivalent of something out of *Easy Rider* with the addition of cow-horn handlebars and a banana saddle and stem.

Then again, if you'd have put that question to me in 1975, I'd have either said hearing Stevie Wonder's ground-breaking *Songs in the key of life* LP or even better losing my virginity—where my foreplay consisted of shouting 'I'm coming'. I must have given my teenage sweetheart the best ten seconds she's ever had! And at 18 the most memorable thing was seeing my journalistic byline name in print for the first time on the regional press front page splash 'Nazis recruiting in town'—a special report by Paul Wellings. But music was my sanctuary, as the sweet soul song said. In fact, music had been my life since I was ten, and if it wasn't for Rock against Racism festivals with bands like Steel Pulse and reading the NME in the seventies, I would never have been politicised.

Unlike most pop journalists I didn't want to be in a band (I'd signed a record deal a year before through the Mad Professor's reggae label Ariwa with my band the Anti Social Workers, and the LP *Positive Style* got glowing reviews in all the music press and we toured at venues like the Hammersmith Odeon with reggae legends Peter Tosh and Eek A Mouse. So that was out of my system), and I didn't want to be a pop PR or do drugs with Lemmy. Amusingly, the Anti Social Workers toured with other pop writers from the music press on benefit gigs for the miners, printers *et al.* These included the Redskins (Chris 'X' Moore from the NME), Attila the Stockbroker (John Opposition from Sounds) and Seething Wells (Steven Wells from the NME) as well as supporting the usual suspects such as Billy Bragg, New Model Army, 3 Johns and Benjamin Zephaniah, and we all reviewed each other unashamedly as the loofah to the Thatcherite scourge. Talk about power, corruption, lies and gratuitous nepotism. John Opposition from Sounds said: 'It's time that someone managed to cross over and equally appeal to the punk and reggae audiences, and the Anti Social Workers may just be the band to do it.' Steven Wells from the NME wrote: 'The Anti Social workers jumped from Poland's failed revolution to abusing the alleged Robert Elms in the time-honoured fashion of the Socialist anti-pose.' X Moore from the NME concluded: 'Positive Style is an album set apart.' Sean O'Hagan, NME: 'The Anti Social Workers' lauded first LP', or Gaye Abandon, NME: 'The Anti Social Workers, four young persons of various cult persuasions, had the novel idea of singing and toasting over tasty dub tracks courtesy of the Mad Professor.'

I last saw X Moore in 1997 outside 10 Downing Street when Tony Blair was just coming to power and the PM was arriving. I shook John Prescott's hand and looked behind me and there was X Moore, no longer the public school revolutionary skinhead in DMs and Red Harrington with crop top—but instead looking like Paul Weller *circa* first Style Council album—all long gelled-back hair and raincoat: Apparently he was living in France up to various subversion and I stupidly said to him: 'Now this is real democratic socialism, none of your schoolboy revolutionary politics here,' (thinking Blair was still true Labour) and he sneered: 'We'll see.' And he was right—as phoney Tony and his cronies were to prove. Although I had no truck with X Moore's Trotskyism (which seemed to be for over-educated wussies), my brand of socialism had never wanted to overthrow capitalism. All I wanted was what all decent-minded people wanted—fairer distribution of wealth through taxation, free health care at the point of need; the provision of decent affordable housing for all; and free education up to university level. These were fairly modest demands. But for the first time in Britain's history a majority of public opinion finds itself to the left of a Labour government (which just means in the centre)—on issues from pensions protection and taking railways back into public ownership to curbing fat cat greed and keeping the health service in public hands.

Large numbers oppose the government's support for Bush's seemingly endless war programme and are ashamed that this is the first Labour government under which the gap between rich and poor has increased rather than shrunk. Nor do most people think it is right that workers can be sacked for taking lawful industrial action and that British employees have fewer rights at work than anywhere else in Europe. Under Blair we live in a time when the gap between haves and have-nots has never been greater; When the number of strikes is the lowest since records began; When millions who live on the bare minimum are no longer unionised; When the notion of an effective 'labour movement' is already history; When social democrats plan the alienation of the working class; When the idea of equal opportunities is exploited to obscure social division; When the level of race attacks has been likened to political terrorism; When political support for the European far-right is gauged in millions. And when despite everything, the left still tells us 'there is no better time to be a socialist' to whom do we turn? I genuinely don't know because they're all liars and cheats!

But as Garry Johnson, a former *Sounds* music journalist colleague of mine, wisely said, 'All we have to remember is we have more in common with the black working class than the white middle class.' In my view it is either socialism or barbarism—and going through life like all independent, free-thinking people with that optimism of the will and pessismism of the intellect. I wanted the same dream as Jonathan Freedland in his excellent account of the British revolution that became America—*Bring Home the Revolution*—when he talks about the things this country urgently needs such as popular sovereignty; more democracy; a new republic; a culture of rights; a written constitution; local power; civil society; the classless society and a new British identity. X Moore (like all the NME staff) also didn't like my notion of 'Enlightened Patriotism' influenced by Orwell's accounts of 'socialism and the English genius'. I was proud of this country and its working class traditions and believed you could have patriotism without prejudice. I wanted to reclaim the St George cross that had been hijacked by fascists and introduce 'Jerusalem' as our national anthem (rather than that anachronistic dirge 'God

Save The Queen' which alongside the House of Lords and our public school system is still creating a 'them and us' society) and show that you didn't need to be a xenophobic neanderthal redneck with your knuckles dragging along the ground to be a patriot: you could have patriotism with intelligence. It was the kind of view that people like Billy Bragg are pioneering now and are still meeting resistance to (so imagine the grief I got in 1983!).

I was talking about that particular strain of Englishness that runs from George Orwell to Tony Benn; from the Sex Pistols to Ms Dynamite. I wanted to reclaim that notion of Englishness which has been turned from a shared identity and solidarity into a political weapon for racists. Billy Bragg summed it up when he said to *The Guardian:* 'The Scots seem to have a certain amount of confidence on who they are, but the paradox for us in England is that on the one hand, we're the most culturally diverse country in Europe, and yet we're the most afraid. We have this fear that we're about to be swallowed up by European culture.

'Look at the strength we've got from that diversity—and that diversity goes right back to the Anglo-Saxons. The only native English bit of that name is the hyphen.

'Englishness can only be defined by the borders of the country,' he concludes. 'I'm not interested in a narrow definition of warm beer and Benjamin Britten. It's about a shared space, and you can't pick and choose within that.'

With this patriotism, ironically I was one of the few people at the NME who had spent most of my life in a multi-cultural community and was deemed by my roughneck black mates 'an honorary brother'. I was not some patronising rich kid WIGGA who do it all for street credibility and slumming. I didn't affect a Jamaican accent but still spoke in my 'posh cockney' estuary English regional accent while understanding all the black patois and speaking it in a crossover fashion. I frequented, with my funki dred friends, exclusively black clubs like the Four Aces in Dalston, DJ'd in non-white clubs such as Trends in Hackney (once getting a replica pistol put to my head before I was accepted) and shopped at all the black designer shops and worked in black record shops in Mare Street, Hackney (where Trevor Nelson used to work and serving DJ customers like Bobbi and Steve from the Kiss Zoo experience). I was in the main treated with respect and dignity. As Michael Moore says in *Stupid White Men*, it's the dumb redneck white guys you've got to watch. When you look back on your life, didn't most of the shit you received come from white people, and come to think of it haven't all the best bosses you've had been women?

I also said something dumber and dumber to former NME politico X Moore like, 'God you've changed—you've become everything you hated,' forgetting I was in a suit and tie. 'Look at *you*,' he replied. He got me again. I blew it and wished I'd treated him with a bit more compassion and humility. Next time I looked over to talk to him, he'd gone.

Steven Wells I saw on an Underground train last year and he had his head buried in a Penguin modern classic and I raised my eyebrows at him in friendship but I don't think he recognised me. To this day I don't know why I didn't speak to him as I always liked him. Attila the Stockbroker I saw at a gig last month and he hasn't changed a bit and had a particularly amusing song about how Phill Jupitus (a mutual ex-chum of ours) had sold out. Jupitus and his idol Jonathan Ross are very funny men but they play on being East End cheeky chappies.

5: Casuals and clubs

ON my days at the NME I would like to tell it how I found it, without fear, favour or score-settling. Call me a self-destructive young fool, but I've always believed in sometimes nibbling at the hand that feeds me. Throughout my journalistic career I've refused to wear the brown lipstick (as sported by Tony Blair after visiting George Bush) and I've been known to launch broadsides against many of my employers. So I was on my best behaviour when I went to the NME for the first time. I remember walking into the office in Carnaby Street in my soulboy 'casual' Aquascutum and Daks gear and realising how old and uncool everyone was. I was the first genuine casual that the NME ever hired as a writer. I believed the casual thing was truly underground and revolutionary. Punk was orchestrated but this was anti-fashion. I first saw it when black chums of mine started wearing Gabicci tops (AKA reggae's Gregory Isaacs). It was the 'sticksman' look where urban, working class faces would gain the clothes and accessories to give them standing with their peers, and they would have to live on society's margins to achieve this 'great look'. Plus you had to be arrogant and resilient to survive on the NME and the casual vibe was all part of this. Talking tough because it was all you had.

By 1980 the skinhead fashion had drifted away from football and a new breed of 'football fashion' had come about. The young men who worked Monday to Friday eight till five, who went to the football at the weekend to get away from it all, now had something else to spend their money on: expensive designer clothing. Not since the Mod era in the sixties had chaps been so concerned about their appearance. Favoured labels in the early days of the casuals were Lacoste, Tacchini, Ellesse, Kappa, Burberry, Lois, Levis, Pringle. Station platforms on Saturdays were packed with young chaps wearing Fila BJ tracksuit tops (these were the official tracksuit top that tennis legend Bjorn Borg used to wear) and Lois cords or a Burberry Harrington jacket with a Daks scarf underneath wrapped high around the neck and a pair of Levis jeans with a pressed-in seam. Most important of all was the choice of footwear: if you didn't wear the correct trainers, you didn't look the part. The Liverpudlians claimed they were the front-runners in fashion as they would pick up the latest styles from abroad on their European trips; they would regularly walk into Lacoste boutiques empty-handed, but come out with a handful of polo shirts and sweaters, obviously with no receipts for any. By the mid to late-eighties the labels were changing, with the expensive sportswear being replaced by designer labels such as Armani, Aquascutum, Chipie and Chevignon but Burberry and Lacoste were still very popular.

Into the nineties casuals continued to wear Lacoste and Burberry; other labels which became popular on the terraces were Ralph Lauren, Paul Smith, CP Company and the label which is probably the most notorious 'casuals' brand to date, Stone Island, which denotes the ugly face of hooliganism. Footwear was still a key factor, with the casuals now swaying away from the favoured sporty trainer look of the eighties, with Timberland shoes being the smarter new look. With this, baseball caps became very popular as a trendy accessory for the casual; much favoured were Timberland and Ralph Lauren. During the nineties the casual scene at football dropped off as attention turned to drugs and music, with bands such as The Stone Roses and The Happy Mondays virtually taking over the 16 to 25-year-old population; everyone wanted to be a part of the 'Madchester' and 'rave' scene. Ecstasy, dubbed the 'happy drug', became widely available and a lot of the boys who once would have run with a casual 'firm' now just wanted to 'dance' or 'chill'. By the mid-nineties the streets were awash with counterfeit designer clothing, the most popular being Ralph Lauren and Timberland; this overkill naturally led to these labels dying out as the leading gear to be seen in. Towards the end of the nineties Burberry had begun to become ever more popular, with the 'house check' check shirt being the favourite. The other popular item at this time were Rockport boots, as these had taken over from Timberland shoes as the *de rigueur* footwear.

In the 21st century casuals still exist up and down the country, with chaps still splashing out hundreds of pounds on flash designer clothing. Somewhere between the year 2000 and 2001 Burberry seemed to explode and was seen on every street corner, the most popular item being the 'house check' baseball cap. These were relaunched in mass production, so the exclusivity was now gone and a lot of the casuals didn't want to be seen in them: Another label which became very big was Hackett: at the European Championships 2000, virtually every other England fan in Belgium was wearing a Hackett polo shirt, the most popular being the ones with the St George's cross on them. With this overkill, the Hackett fad died out within a year or so. Favoured labels with today's casuals are Aquascutum, Armani, CP Company, Paul & Shark, Burberry and above all Stone Island: the expensive Italian designer sportswear with the famous button-on sleeve badge is still the top label amongst the more thuggish casuals. Footwear has again changed; gone are the Rockport boots of the late nineties, replaced by Campers, Clarks Originals, Timberland Boots and a lot of Adidas 'old skool' trainers similar to the styles from the eighties. After the quieter spell of the nineties it would seem as though the 'casuals' fashion has become very popular; there are many guys at football grounds across the country dressed head-to-toe in designer clothing. Many of these are just very young naïve lads who just look the part, but as in the eighties they are using football matches as a catwalk, trying to out-dress each other. Not only are there the young casuals at today's grounds, but a lot of the one-time young casuals of the eighties now are thirty/fortysomething professional men, in their expensive designer clothing, leading by example. Less is more for the genuine casuals—with only a miniscule label or just a tiny badge on the sleeve with a colour on it (no name) or French Connection Hawaian shirts and linen shorts with boating shoes—while the hooligan element swagger around in their garish Burberry and Hackett shirts. A little tip: Always avoid people in Burberry, Stone Island and Hackett shirts—as they're reactionary meatheads. Soccer casuals are not just a fad or a fashion; they never were—it's a Culture. Even Tony Blair wears Paul Smith.

In the seventies, taking the cover of Bowie's *Young Americans* as a point of reference, casuals had combined the bohemian cool of Bowie with punk's smarter trappings. The resulting image was aggressive, effeminate and extremely attractive. Mohairs worn with straights and plastic sandals, rounded off by camel duffel coats. But it was the distinctive hairstyle that stamped soulboy casual all over them, the unique and wonderful lopsided wedge—a haircut popular in the last great depression, ludicrously 'claimed' by hair stylist Trevor Sorbie at Vidal Sassoon Salon.

The start of the 1977 football season saw this look spreading, slowly at first, while a thriving club scene began to take shape. It was around February of 1978 that this fledgling fashion shook off its punk roots and became more of a cult, a football-orientated lifestyle. Suddenly everyone at the match was sporting a drooping fringe, straights and Pod shoes. Though drinking, stealing, fucking and clubbing were all important, obsession with clothes gripped young Londoners and Scousers with a vengeance. But even though all discerning Londoners had been buying their clothes from sports shops like Lillywhites since the days of Bertie Wooster—we all thought a label would change our lives—it didn't. Between spring 1978 and winter 1979 the emphasis went on detail. It was a new label every month. Inega, Fiorucci, Lacoste, FUs all had their moments, but never very long ones. Now this was fashion. No sooner was a new brand or colour established than it was cast off, replaced for fear of ridicule.

As 1979 wore on, though, ideas were thin on the ground. The style leaders simply went more ridiculous, by wearing no underpants, walking with their hands behind their backs and using Staffordshire Bull Terriers

28

as a fashion appendage. Then the mad hatters arrive. All manner of headgear came and went: baseball caps, deerstalkers, trappers' hats, flat caps. By this time the cult was well established.

Towards the end of the seventies Joy Division's 'Love will tear us apart' could be heard next to The Crusaders' 'Street Life', and it was this leaning towards jazz-fusion that prompted a renewed interest in quality. However, the Londoners could not be beaten at their own game and the Chaps came up with a luxurious image unlike anything touched upon before. This was an incongruous mixture of Nike trainers, frayed Lois jeans and Lacoste shirts, worn with Aquascutum cashmere scarves and Lyle and Scott golfing jumpers, topped with long beige Burberry raincoats. The age of football terrace chic was with us. But 1980 saw a change in direction. Long fringes were replaced by huge, bowl-type mushroom wedges, instantly doubling the width of the head. At the same time the clothing was much more sports-conscious, rather than club-orientated.

The Londoners displayed a variety of leatherwear and Lacoste yellow and pink jumpers before knuckling down to the serious business of out-sporting the world with Head and Barbour. By 1981 just about every team in the country was able to boast a collection of match ace faces, each trying to outdo the next city in terms of terrace chic.

That was the background to the casuals. Whatever happens in the future, I maintain that there are few finer moments in life than when you step into an alien city *en masse*, dressed to the nines, and watch those people stare. Ted Polhemus in an article on street style wrote: 'The football terrace is a place where street styles are born and bred.'

The rise of the casuals matched the rise of Margaret Thatcher. Indeed, many say the former were the ultimate expression of the latter's philosophy. Pulling themselves up by their bootstraps with free enterprise, always flying the flag, giving short shrift to the liberals and moaning minnies, the casuals gave Thatcherism its most literal interpretation. Except they were multi-cultural and loved black music—not something for Maggie's Farm.

Their golden age ended, however, before the Iron Lady was given the boot. Some say it was the age of rave and too much ecstasy which distracted the casuals from their perfection of sportswear chic. Others point to the tragedy which took place at the Heysel Stadium in Belgium in 1985 and which brought to an end the casuals' sporting/shopping expeditions on the Continent, where they saw Italian and French fans and thought they were models straight off the catwalk. English fans looked second-class citizens in comparison. Though I find it hard to find much affection for the casuals nowadays (marred by the violence, did their movement ever extend much beyond going for ludicrously over-priced clobber?), it must be said that their influence has been immeasurable. Not only did they help Rave on its way, they also paved the way for the meteoric success of firms like Ralph Lauren and Stone Island in the 1990s. More than this, however, they produced a long overdue British men's style revolution. That sharpness of dress and brain, and consummate attention to detail, which characterised the early Mods (and, it should be said, many skinheads) had been lost in the late seventies. Like the Mods before them, the casuals turned Britain on to quality European menswear and, in their own way, helped to make men more open to the narcissistic pleasures of the style wars.

The casual movement can be seen as a working class response to a seismic shift in wider society: just as the Mods copied their bosses and demanded the best so the casuals aspired to designer status. Their philosophy was summed up best in Paolo Hewitt's book *Soul Stylists* when he said: 'You may come from nothing but you will go to every length to dress like you have everything.'

When I interviewed playwright and top casual Mick Mahoney for the NME, he showed me how to dress differently; otherwise you were a walking advert as a thief. I would shop at Moda on Tower Bridge Road, Stuarts in Acton and Daks. I would later form the only dance-based casual band with Mick called 'The Diamond Gang' which I blagged a session on Capital Radio for by writing about them under a pseudonym. Paolo Hewitt told me he heard the session in a cab and told the cab driver to stop while he listened to it—because he'd read all the hype about them and not known it was my band.

Mick Mahoney was the coolest guy I'd ever seen and a very influential writer for me. Shannon's 'Let The Music Play' and Cheryl Lynn's 'Encore' were the soundtrack and we had the clothes—we could dress to impress. The casual scene developed into the urban R'n'B and hip hop scene you see today with the dubious 'pop a cap in you' culture, 'bling bling' champagne lifestyle and clothes from Agnes B, Prada, Gucci, Evisu and elite Japanese designers like Osaki.

I believed in the old Mod ethic 'smart living in difficult circumstances' while the NME staff believed in 'shabby living in comfortable circumstances'. They all seemed to have the dress sense of Worzel Gummidge. But contrary to their blinkered view of casuals, I didn't cling on to the ideas of bullying and bigotry that were to taint the movement. When the *Sun* and all the monosyllabic goons caught on to casuals, you knew it would be all about basic principles—such as fuck everyone else and look after yourself, be greedy, sneer at anything remotely socialist as it was considered the politics of the weak. Strictly for Jeremy Punk from

Hampstead. This is what filtered down to the boys on the dole queue and the kids in the playground with their silly Fila tracksuits.

As the cut-throat eighties turned into the caring, sharing nineties and the casual was now a thirtysomething, suddenly compassion started replacing cynicism. The 1991 Summer of Love led to football thugs from rivals West Ham and Millwall dropping Es and kissing each other on the dance floor in New Cross Warehouse parties. The chemical generation had arrived. I went along in a full-on, loved-up way with this. To follow was Oasis, great chap films like Justin Kerrigan's *Human Traffic* and the Post Di phenomenon and the Blair Project. The eventual conclusion of all this at the turn of the century was New Years' Eve 1999—people partying like it was 1944. Immortal lines from Dagenham street parties like my father-in-law saying: 'The fireworks are like the Blitz but no-one gets killed this time.'

And when the chaps started voting for the rebel Ken Livingstone for Mayor of London, you knew the life cycle had gone full circle. I was now in my mid-thirties and mellowed with two babies and a loving wife. I remembered Ibiza's Café Del Mar (where our LWR crew had DJ'd) and laughed at the stylised violence of Tarantino like 'we'll execute the fucking lot of you, won't we, honey bunny?' In a stream of unconsciousness we casual chaps were the lucky, lucky people. We were legends in our own egos. From the UK garage and R'n'B scenes to the Rockport shirts, we were complete hedonists with absolute mistresses. We were quicker on the draw than Jesse James. It was spiritual.

The media loved the rise and rise of the casuals—and a by-product was our first casual Prime Minister Tony Blair, with his Ralph Lauren tennis shirts and designer casual children in their Ted Baker shirts spilling over their Valentino jeans. Very terrace fashion. Writer Anna Battista agreed with my buddy Kevin Sampson that the government was still no closer to understanding the phenomenon now than it was 20 years ago in spite of Tony Blair's casual dress.

6: Proles and goals

IN the early eighties at the NME media bunker, none of the staff seemed to appreciate the greatness of black music and black culture the way I did. They probably thought 'the Philly Sound' was a young female horse trotting. I've always believed that confidence with a dash of arrogance is a fine quality so it's fair to say I didn't think any of them was a better pop writer than me.

George Orwell once said about England that it was 'the most class-ridden country under the sun. It is full of snobbery and privilege and ruled by the old and the silly.' That perfectly describes the NME at that time. They didn't understand the working class attitude that 'we don't want to be middle-class, we want to be rich'. I had all the horny-handed son of toil credentials: I didn't have my coal in the bath, I had it in the bidet. I came from peasant stock and unlike virtually anyone on the NME wasn't a weak liberal but a strong socialist, didn't go to public school or university and loved shagging and drinking with a passion. The rest were like men behaving sadly. Rebels without a clue.

I didn't get work there because I was any good (I worked my way through Burchill's and Parsons' style adequately), but because they were just really bad. No-one had replaced the loss of Burchill (the most talented writer the pop press ever had), Danny Baker and Mr Parsons. Even the lovely pussycat Paolo Hewitt, their resident soulhead, had a Fred Perry and a Harrington jacket on (which no self-respecting urban soulie would have been seen dead in at the time). Paolo made a name for himself as Paul Weller's sidekick—but much of the mythology about Weller shattered for me when I interviewed him and he was the one of the shiest, most tongue-tied people I'd ever met, but one of the greatest British singer/ songwriters ever (right up there with John Lennon and Ray Davies).

The only people I had any real affinity with seemed to be the beautiful girls in reception, who I shared many laughs with—especially about the phrase 'going round the world': a sublime sexual act (allegedly).

Without wishing to sound prolier-than-thou, I suppose the rantings of a 19-year-old kid from a housing association in the London new towns stood out considerably, considering the NME's reader profile: very pale, male and stale. But of course I was noticed. I was the nearest thing they'd seen to a working-class kid since Burchill, Parsons and Baker (who were from even more humble backgrounds than mine).

When I walked into the office in my soccer casual uniform, they looked scared, as if I was a hooligan or a thief or both (I was actually a pussycat but I let them sweat). They all kept their hands on their wallets when I walked in. I was the real deal. I told the features editor Tony Stewart that he wasn't writing about anything that anyone my age was interested in. When I got an exclusive which became the NME front-page splash, on Jimmy White the snooker superstar, Tony insisted he and Paolo help me write the questions and I just do the interview—even though I had far more journalistic qualifications than those two put together.

The NME's legendary writer Nick Kent, who always said yes to excess, once wrote: 'Loud music made by self-destructive white boys was what I wanted to write about. The Stones, The Stooges, the New York Dolls. I wasn't interested in temperance, I was devoured by rock 'n' roll. I wasn't interested in Lord Byron, as I was hanging out with the Byron of the seventies, Keith Richards. I wanted to speak up for the counter-culture—this was life in the extreme.' Kent was one of the many NME people who in true Spinal Tap style wanted to turn it up to 11. He once said: 'At the age of 19 I started smoking hashish in earnest, and then moved on to speed and cocaine. Finally I was offered some heroin and that was it for me. It was like being in heaven, it was ecstasy. I thought this was worth getting lost for. I was on a death trip—I was into smack, cocaine, Valium, all kinds of things. If I hadn't got myself off I would be into crack by now. I should be insane or dead.' Neil Spencer, talking about record company launches, told the ever-stylish Dylan Jones (of GQ fame): 'You saw the most appalling things; every music critic in London seemed to take it for granted that they had to behave as disreputably as possible.' Journalists would often start fights with each other, pinch each other's drugs and verbally abuse any rock star who came near them. Apparently one female journalist only agreed to interview Iggy Pop on the understanding he hit on her (which he duly did), while another asked to see a famous rock guitarist's cock only to get a pistol in her mouth. But Frank Zappa summed it up best by calling music journalism 'stuff written by people who can't write, about people who can't speak, for people who can't read'.

Nick Cohn, author of the beautifully written *Awopbopalloobop Awhambamboom*—the first rock 'bible'—said: 'Not having been to a place never stopped me from describing it. Anymore than not meeting someone stopped me talking about my interview with them.' Cohn's 'Tribal Nights of the New Saturday Night' in *New York* magazine was to shape the enduring film *Saturday Night Fever*—a must for any soul boy like me.

My first job interview with NME editor Spencer (who seemed to share my love of black culture especially reggae but from a more theoretical perspective) was more a 'portrait of the journo as a consumer' with me listing my favourite film, record and book: in case you're interested it was *Blue Collar*, *What's Going On* and *Brighton Rock*. Neil, probably the only spliff-loving new age hippy I've ever liked a lot, decided to introduce me to the delights of his video collection with Nicolas Roeg's *Performance* and GF Newman's *Law and Order* (I'd seen both before on TV but went along with his well-intentioned *Educating Rita* routine). He was right to remind me of these classics because they remain two of my favourites to this day.

Up I went again for the second interview, again with Neil. More music questions, but this time a formality because I'd come recommended by Tony Parsons—what better recommendation do you need?

'So, umm. . . what groups do you like?'

'I love Cameo, Maze, Leroy Hutson, Millie Jackson, Gil Scot Heron. My favourite record is "Cross the Tracks" by Maceo and the Macks (something that changes every year for me).' He seemed quite pleased with that response and gave a toothy grin.

He remembered that he was Neil Spencer, of the world's best-selling pop music magazine, too smooth to move. 'You got the job,' he said—I was to become their ace stringer. Neil went on to describe my work as 'From sports stars, to actors to gangsters—if you ever wondered what London's own Lower East Side is like, enquire within.'

I was confident. I knew soul music inside out—I was going to clubs and listening to pirate radio stations that no-one else on the NME was aware of (except for the other great stringer and DJ Dave Dorrell who went on to found the chart-topping group MARRS, famous for 'Pump Up The Volume' and at whose house I ended up staying over on occasions and borrowing his books). At last I would be a somebody. Yes, I would be the first journo to visit nasty gangland boss Reggie Kray at Parkhurst Prison, a man with the hardest handshake I'd ever felt and with such a menacing charisma and who ripped up my notes at one stage with a grin, but I lived to tell the tale; yes, I would do an interview with Ian Dury while he was on his exercise bike and discover he was every bit as funny and humanitarian as his punk poet-laureate status lyrics showed; in fact, he had rhyming couplets on his walls for unfinished songs and the biggest collection of reference books on the English language I've ever witnessed. Dury suffered for his art; yes I would interview big bad Barry White and he would say 'I want a picture of you and me together'; and soul songstress Natalie Cole would give me a smile during an interview to make traffic stop, even though she had just gone through her own drink/drugs heaven/hell (delete where appropriate) and was completely unaware of the underground status and value of some of her 'rare groove' tunes in the UK.

I had made something out of nothing. I was going to be a real writer. I had arrived. Everything was for the best in the best of all possible worlds. I soon realised that writing for the pop papers was not listing what tracks a band played but writing about what interested you at the concert. Danny Baker once wrote a whole feature on Michael Jackson talking about his flight to Los Angeles and didn't mention the music at all (I met Jackson at Madame Tussaud's with the immortal interview line 'Michael—do you think you've got more wax on your face than the dummy nowadays?'—'uh I don't think so'. I also heard that Baker once waited for Ian Penman with a chair leg after he called him 'a boil on the bottom of beat music', so there was a lot of friction. Baker actually made up the first-ever Paul Weller interview and Sham 69's interview because he was too lazy to arrange it—I admired that.

The most important thing I learnt about pop writing was after interviewing Danny Baker when he instructed me to write what you enjoy—rock journalism is not writing about tracks on albums: 'If you saw something funny on the TV, then write about that and say the band were crap.' Sadly I was to blow my friendship with Danny in many ways but mainly by getting 'tired and emotional' at the LWT studios, where he used to invite me up to the 6 O'Clock Show every Friday, and upsetting one of the top suits up there. Baker took me for drinks with his mum and dad on Surrey Docks and around the supermarkets with him (where he is quite a fast, efficient shopper—maybe he should go on Supermarket Sweep—he'd clean up). Baker was always the ultimate old person's young person. He still scoffs at convention, and that's mighty fine and dandy. But he definitely has a face for radio.

All this led me to understand that journalism must subscribe to the mushroom theory: not that you're a fun guy but you're often left in the dark and get shit thrown at you.

But without Tony Parsons none of this would have been possible. Meeting him for the first time was memorable. The interview went something like this:

PW: How about a brief life history?

TP: Daddy was a banker, and mummy was a racehorse ... only kidding. Southern, working-class, father an ex-Royal Marine Commando who won the Distinguished Service Medal—Julie reckons that I think anyone who didn't fight in the Second World War should feel guilty and I think she's probably right. I started writing stories when I was nine—sub-James Bond ripping yarns featuring a rock-jawed hero called Matt Dagger, and each week I would pin a new episode on the noticeboard at school—the teachers thought I was being creative, but I was just showing off. I passed my eleven-plus (mine was the last year to take it) but left school at sixteen and got a job on Stave Wharf in London docks. Bummed around Europe a few times, worked in a number of jobs—computer operator, fruit importer, gin distillery drone—wrote a novel, sold that novel to the NME when they asked for 'Hip Young Gunslingers' ... I got one job, Julie got the other. We started the same day sharing an office. That was when we met.

PW: What made you become a music writer?

TP: Nobody else would have me. Not that I tried very hard—Fleet Street, local rags, the alternatives to the music press were too gruesome to contemplate. I wanted to earn my living writing and it was better than working for Gordon's Gin and it was *the* time to be a music writer for me. I mean, I set eyes on the Sex Pistols months before I saw the editorial office of the NME.

PW: What was the interview like you did for the job?

TP: A screen test. I just had to be myself—or what I was then, in 1976—and it was just what they were looking for. Our Punk Correspondent.

PW: I think punk produced the best writers to ever work on the music press. Do you agree and why was that?

TP: I agree to a certain extent. There was a lot more to react to in those days—doing the first live Jam review, reviewing the first Clash album, covering the Pistols' Jubilee Day boat trip busted up by the police. What have people got to react to today? U2? The Alarm? How can a young journalist cut his teeth on that bilge?

PW: Do you think there are many writers coming through from working class backgrounds?

TP: As many as there were. Probably more.

PW: What do you think of the state of the music press now?

TP: The papers don't sell enough. When I was on the staff of the NME we sold around a quarter of a million copies each and every week. Now the sales are down to 140,000 a week for NME and considerably less for the others. The music press should be stronger because, if it is not, the music business will not be afraid of it and it should be afraid of it. Otherwise you are just another trade paper in another boring little business.

PW: Why do you still contribute to NME?

TP: Because I love the NME.

PW: But the readers are liberal wallies, a 100 per cent university student audience (like most of the writers).

TP: I didn't say I loved the readers.

PW: What is the favourite jape you pulled up at the NME (apart from you and Julie snorting speed off the editor's desk)?

TP: Iggy Pop dropped in trying to cadge some drugs. We gave him laxatives that he took to be speed pills. He gulped the lot down and gave himself the running squirts, had to keep diving behind the amps and speakers when he was on stage that night at the Rainbow to go to the toilet. They banned him after that. That was pretty funny.

PW: A lot of people I've spoken to, Tony, said you were as sharp as a knife and wouldn't take any shit from anyone—was that the way to survive in that job?

TP: Not really. Being a rock writer is a very, very easy job. It doesn't take much surviving; it's not like being a mine worker or a Sandinista guerilla or something.

PW: Julie Burchill has been attacked as being a conservative waving a left flag—ie, her views on capital punishment, anti-Solidarnosc etc. Do you have sharp differences of opinion?

TP: No, I believe in hanging Lech Walesa myself!

PW: How have you changed since writing *The Boy Looked At Johnny*? It's something of a bible to rock writing now.

TP: I am five years older and probably a lot more tolerant now. After all, there's not much sense in persecuting some hapless little rock band as if they were the South African police force. But I wouldn't change a thing—apart from the dedication to Menachem Begin, which was a mistake—because the book is so funny. It's still selling, you know, and last year it was published in Germany and Greece. I'm stunned at how it has run and run—*The Mousetrap* of rock writing more than the bible, I think.

PW: What made you join the Labour Party?

TP: I realised that moaning about how scummy Thatcher is was not enough. I joined the Labour Party because, to quote our Prime Minister, there is no alternative.

PW: Are you active in the Labour Party?

TP: I attend meetings, I canvass votes, leaflet and campaign in local, national and European elections, I collect stuff for jumble sales and try to recruit sympatico souls. I'm active.

PW: What do you think of the left-wing splinter groups?

TP: I think they are irrelevant, misguided, living in cloud cuckoo land ... I don't think much of them. There is only the Labour Party. And if the Labour Party does not win the next election then it will mean that neither Callaghan, Foot or Kinnock could defeat Thatcher and the Labour Party will be all washed up. So the Labour Party must win the next election.

PW: What advice would you give to up and coming writers about polemical writing?

TP: Spouting somebody's manifesto is no substitute for real passion.

PW: Which music writers do you admire?

TP: Don Watson, Gavin Martin, Paolo Hewitt, Chris Bohn, Paul Du Noyer—the NME has the strongest staff it has had for eight years—it is a shame there is not much for them to write about.

PW: Why did you move into writing books? Was the music press too trivial?

TP: Not at all—the music press is only trivial if you're a trivial writer, and there are plenty of them. I moved into writing books because I felt I had given it long enough on the rock press and it was time to move over, move on and try something fresh. When we quit our staff jobs, I was 25 and Julie was 19. I chose to write books because having 500 pages all to myself, being left alone for months on end by editorial advisers, seeing a massive gap in the market for the books I wanted to write ... how could I resist it?

I met him at his bungalow in Radford Court, Billericay in the sleepy Essex suburbs, an area where Tony was raised. He was the original Billericay Dickie, not a bleeding thickie and doing very well. He would later take me round to his parents, when he wanted his laundry done, to the house he grew up in as a kid.

His mum and dad were as witty, intelligent and charming as Tony. These were good people. My own mum, a miners' daughter and a school assistant, would have got on famously with Tony's mum. Tony extended his big hand. He was a young man of above medium height and what only can be described as a 'bit of a sort' for the ladies. On entering Tony's house he sat me down asked if I wanted food (and went out and generously bought the most expensive Chinese takeaway imaginable) and we did a great interview (extracts from which you've just read). Surprisingly, he described his favourite record as the *Guys and Dolls* soundtrack and his favourite book as *Midnight Cowboy*. After which we all played Star Wars running around with light sabres with his son Robert (from the marriage with Julie Burchill, who had walked out of this house just prior to my visit). Tony made me laugh uncontrollably and he didn't stop making me do that for the next 12 years. Whether it was me following him gleefully through the bookshops in the Charing Cross Road, him waiting for me for an hour at Liverpool Street station (real loyalty) or the registrar at my small wedding asking Tony for the rings—in sorrow and in joy from this day forward—he brought a bit of magic to my life.

Being a nosy little rascal, I browsed through his record collection which contained an abundance of Springsteen and Prince and his bookcase which contained everything from *Crime Inc,* the story of organised crime by Martin Short, to everything by that 'Muhammad Ali of literature'—Norman Mailer (an absolute two-fisted inventive hero to Parsons who to this day has a photo of the man on his study desk). Seeing my curiosity, Tony magnanimously reached down to his bookshelf and gave me his copy of Charlie Gillett's classic history of popular music *Sound of the City* and said: 'This is the bible for pop writers!—just read that.' I did and it remains a valuable reference work to this day.

When I asked him 'the question on everyone's lips is are you a lover or a fighter?', he chuckled and said 'is that really the question on EVERYONE's lips? I wasn't the hardest, cleverest or funniest kid at school. But I was hard, funny and clever.' I could really identify with that. He was aggressive but yet sensitive and at the age of twenty I wanted to be Tony Parsons. He was, it must be said, *even more* working class, than me. My sweet grey-haired old mother, who had the most immaculate working class credentials I've ever known, with no qualifications to her name, was to become an expert on opera and classical music. I once spoke about this to Janet Street Porter who said she was the same—a working class grammar school girl who found a love for opera and art and was never one to take 'pride in ignorance'—probably the biggest weakness of the underclass.

Whenever I marched into the NME, I thought I was Parsons and felt fearless. His first letter to me fired me up: 'Advice for freelancers—push as hard as possible for work without making them feel they are in physical danger if they don't give it to you. Also, act in demand—maybe you should ask Eric Fuller if it is ok if you do some work for *The Face*. Make them feel as though you are wanted elsewhere.

'You get better features and reviews by making the stuff that is appearing under your name SHINE. Work really hard at it—make people want to read everything that has your name on it. When you are an old fogey like me, then you can afford to relax a little. But as someone says in *Winners and Losers*, these are not your resting years. I have never bothered with National Insurance stamps—but, if you don't buy them, don't ever try claiming the dole—but the taxman is another matter. Never annoy the taxman. If they get it in for you, they can be as mean as hell. But don't break a leg trying to pay them—let them come to you, and when they do, play it straight with them. And try this—get a few friends of yours to write about you (they obviously pretend not to know you) to the letters page. Have some of the letters hating you, some loving you, but all with a strong reaction. And work real, real hard at your writing.'

In various letters to me Tony said about me joining the NME: 'Spencer really likes you and this is good news. This is good advice—work your ass off for the NME. You will never regret it. Work your tail off, show them what you can do and you will be rewarded. I have faith in you. I predict a staff job by the end of 1985. Don't let me down. But, much more importantly, don't let yourself down. You got it—use it. This is your chance—take it. I know you can and you will. Your Pal, Tone. PS: your real name would make a good by-line. You are going to have to start using it sooner or later. Why not now? Fuck the DHSS.'

So I entered the NME with tons of attitude all because of Tony Parsons. I started with the bizarre pseudonym Terry Malloy (the character Brando played in a favourite movie of mine *On the Waterfront*) before deciding on Paul Kix, a handle which was a pale imitation of a very pale imitator, Adrian Thrills. But I was never to be a 'star' journalist—just a humble hack fighting for truth, justice and the NME way.

7: Making friends and infuriating people

SUDDENLY 'celebrities' started to write to me at the paper: Scary gangster Reggie Kray said: 'I hope to see you on your own, unless you need to have someone with you. This is not meant to be disrespectful to your friend. God Bless. Reg Kray.' He was referring to the greatest living lensman Lawrence Watson (Paul Weller's favourite photographer and mine, taking great wedding pics of me, my wife and my best man Tony Parsons). Lawrence and I had had an abortive mission to see him in Parkhurst maximum security prison, where we were stripped of all tape recorders and camera. My second visit was with his brother Charlie Kray. (As a rule I get on reasonably well with gangsters, although I know they are throughly nasty people. Charlie, the most charming of the brothers, once gave me his mobile number, saying if I ever needed anyone 'sorted out' I was to give him a bell. I guess I am drawn inevitably towards badness like a junkie to their crack pipe.) Reggie Kray then wrote to me to 'get my two friends in the magazine' who were Geraldine and Janice from Fulham who ran Ratbags Disco Inc (Music for Pleasure)—not exactly NME material.

Billy Bragg, the big-nosed bard from Barking, said: 'Thanks for the review. Your points about some other instrumentation were being dealt with by us as you wrote them, for by Victoria Palace (last night of the tour) I had Dave Woodhead with me supplying trumpet on "The Saturday Boy" and "Man In The Iron Mask" and Bobby Valentino, fiddle player in the Wangfords, doing a fine and soulful job on your own "A Lover Sings". From the first night to the last, a fun tour. I'm sure a persistent little herbert like you will be able to prise a word out of the Redskins. Good luck with the new improved Anti Social Workers. All the best Billy. PS, Your typing is terrible.'

Author Kevin Sampson said about a feature I'd written: 'Brilliant stuff—the most important social commentary of the last 20 years,' which was incredibly flattering and undeserved, I feel. His novels remain some of my favourites to this day. His book *Powder*, based on him being the manager of indie favourites The Farm, was one of the most authentic novels about the mad, mad, mad world of the music business.

With Glen Murphy from *London's Burning*, I played in the TV Entertainers' Celebrity Football Team (I was strictly Z-level celebrity) alongside Ray Winstone, Perry Fenwick, Nick Berry, and Adam Woodyatt. Going around the country with those chaps really was like being in the Rat Pack with its hedonistic pleasures—in fact, they were labelled the Brit Pack (a tilt at the Brat Pack of the time which included Emilio Estevez, Rob Lowe etc). I used to go to Ray Winstone's maisonette in Enfield quite a bit, where he'd be reading the *Sun* (very dubious) and watching films like *The Blues Brothers*. His daughter would paint pictures of me for presents. But I didn't like Ray's, in my view, more redneck views on life and although I thought he was one of the finest British actors (in films such as *Scum, Nil By Mouth* and *Sexy Beast*) I soon stopped seeing him. Actors are all fruitcakes anyway—it's not exactly rocket science or working down a coal mine is it; as Julie Burchill said, 'You just hit your mark and snog someone attractive.' But those football days with the TV entertainers were like the old Frank Sinatra philosophy 'I hope I live till I die'.

I remember coming on the pitch with all these stars and the announcer saying over the Tannoy '...and here is Paul Wellings, presenter with Channel 4', and the crowd saying 'who the fuck is that cunt?—we paid good money to see celebrities.' A blagger to the end. Glen was the only one from that group without an inflated ego and dropped me a line saying, 'Yo Paulie. As promised an East Ender's word is his bond. Hope the hols were great, even fucking great. *London's Burning* is great fun, we are training at Southwark Bridge Road Fire Station. The press have been hassling us, but I told them I'll only speak to Paul Wellings. They seemed nonplussed that actors can do physical tasks, such as training to be firemen. I said talk to THE Paul Wellings, he will tell you how physical I can get, but don't tell the wife. Talk to you later. Big bronzed man. MURF.' Murphy and Winstone went on tape reading my screenplay *Thieves*—but the BBC's Play for Today ran scared of it in the end, saying it was too controversial and the language too strong.

Playwright Barrie Keefe (who wrote the wonderful London gangland movie *The Long Good Friday*) wittily wrote about me changing my *nom de plume*: 'Dear Paul, it came as a great shock to read that the Terry Malloy name is no more. When I last saw the handle (and it seems like only yesterday) it appeared to me to be in the very pink peak of health. So shaken am I by the sudden and unexpected demise, I'm at a total loss to know what to say. However, at the risk of paying a cliché-ridden tribute to a byline that will be sorely missed by so many, I feel compelled to write in grief. TM is gone. But those who knew it will never forget it. The world is a sadder place. In the fullness of time(?) Paul Kix may become a byline to be greeted with as much affection as a name on the newsprint of the NME—perhaps even as big a name. But it will never be as long a name as Terry Malloy. Yours, until the heavens fall.'

Or dubious supercrook Ronnie Biggs writing to me when I worked for *Mojo* for editor Matt Snow, another nice guy from the NME who was in Blair's band Ugly Rumours. 'Thanks for the letter and your comments on *Odd Man Out*. To say that it's only an update of *His Own Story* is all bollocks. I didn't write that book but I did write *Odd Man Out* and I think there's a mile of difference. Anyway it's selling very well indeed and at the end of the day, that's all that matters. One, two, three, four—let us hear the Hammers roar! I've got a mate over here who's a West Ham supporter—you'd love him but I'm an Arsenal fan and always will be. It would be nice to see you and the "struggle" turn up in Rio next year for the 30 years in liberty bash, so start saving your dosh. All the best and my kind of luck.'

Although when you look back at your old work there is a lot to be ashamed about, my favourite bits of my journalism from those days were the following:

My review of *EastEnders* when it screened its first episode: 'The script-writer for *EastEnders* must be a card—the joker in the pack! For the soap characters from Albert Square E20 (where?) would be the life and soul of any funeral. Never before has so much drunken violence been performed by so few brains for so many...

'The programme nearest to capturing the area's atmosphere was Johnny Speight's *Till Death Us Do Part*, set in Wapping. Speight, himself from Canning Town, created in Alf Garnett a hideous relic, an A1 bigot trapped in a two-up, two-downer whose irrational 'it stands to reason' arguments and dumb logic were far more slyly subversive than the way *EastEnders* turns depression into an art form. Moralising switches people off; savage satire hurts... Dr Johnson said that when a man is tired of London, he's tired of life—but if you're tired of life, *EastEnders* is enough to make you top yourself.'

Reviewing Billy Bragg and Elvis Costello at a miners' hardship benefit: 'Next, battered and bruised but never beaten, were the Striking Miners' South Wales Choir. I only wish my nan, a battling miner's wife, had been well enough to see this—it was a truly sublime moment. All it needed was the Beast of Bolsover to introduce them as they sang shoulder to shoulder, taking us from WMC-style solo 'Solitaire' to 'Comrades in Arms' with real stout-hearted vision. "Follow that," someone challenged the man jarringly lodged between Bowie and James Brown in my record collection—young William Steven Bragg, Neither Washington nor Moscow but international Barking (woof, woof). Some say he's a prole for the trendies, a horrendous Right On Sid mutant; others say he's nothing more than an entertaining diversion. I stick by him. With that nose, if he was on hard drugs he'd inhale the whole of Peru. But he can sniff out rich Top Ten hits like "New England", the wishful Top-Ten hit "Between The Wars" (whatsay a Tracey Ullman cover?), or "Times Like These". Trumpeter Dave "Hot Lips" Woodhead, invited up for "Like Soldiers Do", melted magically. A hectic heckler yelled "Bring on Neil Kinnock".

Bragg's cocky retort: "Neil Kinnock doesn't play the trumpet—it keeps falling off the fence!" Choice! Elvis Costello appears to have been over-indulging himself, clock that triple chin ... The old Joe 90 lookalike's set was a strange rag-bag, which suffered from the glaringly absent Afrodiziak and TKO horn backing.

'Don't know about you, blue, but for me the more pacey pieces jangled and jolted in a discordant row—but his glorious crowning attractions were with the mellow, moody "Alison", the aptly titled "Why Do You Throw Dirt In My Face?" and as a third journey back to the stage, a vitriolic, vibrato version of "Shipbuilding"—so emotive, it nearly broke your heart. The miners deserved something THAT special. Later on, as I went East, nearing home, I ignored the *Sun* van unloading today's news; I ignored the planners' dreams gone wrong; I walked proud ... knowing I'd seen more dignity than a Daimler full of bishops.'

The Commodores: 'For a while the Commodores were like the proverbial Koala bear—up a gumtree.'

UK funk: 'Blackfoot (not Beige) UK funk makes me feel like the kid who loves his drunken father—wishes he wasn't drunk but loves him all the same.'

On Phill Jupitus (then known as Porky the Poet): 'Plump Porky the Poet had the goal covered. He's not just big in Stratford—he's big all over. Tons of Fun from the suited-up Joke Centre Clerk, particularly his account of sexually transmitted diseases—which is nothing to clap about!'

Desmond Dekker live: 'The sly cynic in me suspects the only women's movement the Double D is interested in is from the waist down—but like chart acts Laurel and Hardy, Smiley Culture and Lenny Henry, he has done more for race relations than a million Brixton bureaucrats. In fact, there isn't a black geezer I know who hasn't got anything but unshakeable utmost respect for the man ... This man matters.'

Prince: 'But the biggest shock remains Prince, with more slushy sludge than all of them put together. American excess—that'll do no good at all, Your Majesty.'

Gil Scot Heron at the GLC Jobs Festival: 'But forget liberal wet-dreamers flogging a dead Nam war—15 years too late—along came the seer of Poetic Justice Gil Scott Heron. There have been many times when I've found him too right-on and his music lacking in danceability, but he won me over with a much harder suzzed-up four-piece playing with verve and nerves. Heron is agitational organisation as funk dance-track. If only he could release a totally direct single and be a *Top of the Pops* contender in millions of homes. Listen to learn. "Blue Collar", or, inevitably, "Johannesburg": "I hate to see blood flowing, but I'm glad to

44

see resistance growing." He pisses on any putrid punk/politico band you care to name. While the lunatics run the asylum, Heron is part of the solution, not the problem. This man has ANSWERS loud and clear. This ain't really your life ... Seize the Time!'

Millie Jackson: 'Eat it, Eat it. Millie Jackson might have the same surname as Wacko Jacko but she ain't no waxwork dummy. Her show remains a confession box of voracious carnal appetites. And isn't it wonderful to be in the hands and mouth of an expert? ... There's gonna be no 68s tonight, none of this "you give me one and you owe me one" she exclaimed while moving on to her upfront, "no partee, no pussee rap"... They all get slashed with the blade tongue. Women not demanding the right to come—WHACK. Call me a romantic young fool but Millie Jackson comes with a full guarantee—you know you're getting your ear licked by someone special.'

Dancing with Edwin Starr: 'Your itinerant reporter made a proper fool of himself. For he performed a rather unrhythmic can-can alongside Gary "Captain Beaky" Crowley while Edwin Starr sang on the same stage. Bizarre circumstances without a doubt ...'

Soul For Dole Night: 'Over the last two years soul became slightly docile. It lost the edge and urgency that made Martha Reeves want to dance in the street and McFadden and Whitehead say "Ain't No Stopping Us Now". Those tunes were a sweet, hard wall of crunch ready to jump on anything that wasn't nailed down—whereas recently the dance floor had started to have nothing north of the shoulders; too clean, too glossy, too restrained, too beige beat.'

Interviewing Frankie Goes to Hollywood: '*I don't give a **** what Frankie says.* That was one cheeky chappie T-Shirt slogan, designed to crack wry smiles, 'cause it tore through all the horrendous hype, slimy deals, slippery eels and skyscraper egos around me!'

Many of these reviews were totally influenced by staying around Tony's house and hearing his wonderful way with words and the telling phrase.

Tony was the most impressive person I'd ever met. I don't know anyone who wasn't impressed by him. He was hard, funny, radical and intelligent—a PR's wet dream. In my pop press years I met lots of famous people. But not one of them had the magnetism and charisma of Tony. He reminded me of a more sensitive and brighter version of another blue-collar hero of mine, the other Tony from *Saturday Night Fever*, based on working class kids in Brooklyn. He had that swagger and *joie de vivre*. I thought to myself, one day I want to be as good a writer as him.

I used his lines about 'if I had a dog with a face like yours, I'd shave it's arse and teach it to walk backwards quickly' in my first feature for the NME. Tony wrote on the piece when it was printed about some obscure band from Tilbury Docks who I liked: 'Put some work my way when you're editor. Your purple pal, Tone.' Tony had written on the article in purple felt tip pen. It made me feel as proud as when he gave the best man's speech at my wedding and made a toast to 'life, liberty and happiness'. Mr Parsnip, as Julie B calls him, had a way with words. This was the man who people like The Clash and Pistols fawned over—and he was my best friend. Empowerment is not the word.

As opposed to 1976 when pop music was at its dizzy heights, joining the NME in the early eighties was like dying and going to hell. The music was crap except for R'n'B and the greatest number one ever, 'Ghost Town' by The Specials (I'm not prepared to negotiate that point), was a distant memory. The *NME* staff were OK to me to start with, probably thinking that being Tony's best pal made me the editor's blue-eyed boy, which was true. But they soon took offence to my outspoken, authentic views of working class life, underground music and take on sport. It didn't fit in with their cosy liberal (feel sorry for the perpetrator not the underdog victim) mentality and my genuine socialist upbringing.

8: Class—and office—politics

AT FIRST, it must be said, I was in awe of the *NME* staff. But after a while, I understood that they actually were frightened of me. I perfected a sneer and exaggerated swagger from my limited boxing days that put the fear in them. I never apologised or explained (the John Wayne reference again) as that seemed a sign of weakness. I used a cryptic, impenetrable street language combining cockney flypitcher rhyming slang and Yardie black patois that I picked up from the East End bad boys I was going around with—incomprehensible slang like 'Nitto you sigh—she looks Cris' ('Go away you idiot—she looks beautiful'). I got so far inside the counter-culture it was hard to get out—as they say in *The Godfather*, 'Just as you think you're out, they pull you back in.' And as my mum always said, as a kid I would always go for the baddest boy in the class and take them under my wing—I had a real thing for the underdog and nothing had changed.

I was totally boisterous when in the office, totally out of it when outside—and I wasn't exactly filing the scoops. I felt I was getting a bad reputation, I was becoming a stereotypical bogeyman. Certain people at the NME needed to be diced and sliced, which may seem a philistine reaction. I was no monosyllabic goon or neanderthal but I hated people who were disrespectful. I plotted revenge and happy endings. I guess I had too much attitude.

I noticed, just like in showbusiness, that in the rock press there are many people with full-on leather jackets but very few people from humble origins. (Sorry, it's not a working class chip on my shoulder but a whole bag of King Edwards.) Plus loads were class enemies from public school backgrounds such as X Moore—who was a good writer (I thought his feature on the Right to Work marchers was one of the better pieces of the time) but he'd never known real struggle. Nowadays there is absolutely nothing worth reading in the music press—it is like toothpaste. But there was a time when the music press mattered to people, and I was part of that.

I sent bogus letters condemning all my enemies and they clearly did the same. Every picture sells a Tory in the nationals but in the rock press it was still run by hippies. And, as the great man said, you should never trust a hippy. Being naughty by nature I started messing up people's desks and making bogus phone calls. Still, Neil Spencer said I was writing stuff that no-one else could write on that paper. My contacts book was a lot more colourful than the others' little black book of scummy record execs. It was all good, baby. But despite liberating countless records and books to review and then selling them to Cheapo Stevos in Soho for a handsome price, I was not getting all my reviews in print because the mummy-boy establishment had closed ranks on me. I was a bit too real and raw for them and they couldn't stomach it. I remember Paolo Hewitt saying to me: 'I thought that review you wrote on the Leon Griffiths *Minder* book was one of the best things I've read on the underworld and yet they're not using it.' I was becoming *persona non grata*. But I thought about my mates from the tough London new towns with their noses to the grindstone in some factory, and I couldn't help but laugh like a lunatic.

Back home, I played some uplifting soul music from Brother D and the Collective Effort with the lyric 'How we gonna make the nation rise, educate, agitate and organise?', followed by The Jam's finest moment 'Eton Rifles' with the line 'We were no match for their untamed wit'. The music business sucked ass: I was sure of that.

Julie Burchill summed up the music business best as always in her autobiography *I Knew I Was Right* when she said: 'The *men* who work in the music business—be they hacks, DJs or record-label personnel—are groupies of the worst kind, in my experience. They don't even offer honest sex; they offer expense-account booze, or inferior drugs, to any zonked-out muso, however lowly, who will stop and share the moment with them.'

The axe-wielding rocker the Reverend Blair (who loved King Crimson—enough said) wouldn't have been reading the music press at this stage but my favourite quotes or pieces from stories I've written in the press included questioning **Jimmy White** on what he thought about Steve Davis taking part in a young Tory rally. 'That was a bit of a joke, weren't it? Why he was there I don't know; Barry Hearn's probably got a deal with Thatcher or something.'

Edwyn Collins of Orange Juice and my obsession with Jimmy Dean lookalikes: 'Someone told me he looked like James Dean—an old lady with a white stick, dark glasses and a big dog.'

Charlie Kray: 'The twins don't moralise with anyone, they say "we did what we did and they don't make no excuses for it."'

Derek Jameson on being offered the editorship of the *Daily Express*: 'I'm very flattered and delighted but I'm afraid you've got the wrong man—I support the Labour Party.'

Frank Bruno: 'I've got to hit them hard otherwise I'd be back digging dirty great holes in the road.'

Paul Weller: 'I don't care about Nirvana dropping their pants at the MTV awards. I'm past all that bullshit.'

Lilo Ross: 'The doctor told me the ideal height for my weight should be 9ft 2in.'

Robin Williams: 'What's right is what's left if you do everything wrong.'

David Letterman: 'Be suspicious of any doctor who tries to take your temperature with his finger.'

Morrissey on boxing: 'For me it's the sense of glamour that's attractive, the romance, which of course is enormous. But mainly it's the aggression that interests me.'

Woody Allen: 'Sex between a man and a woman can be wonderful—provided you can get between the right man and woman.'

Roseanne Barr: 'Men can read maps better than women, because only the male mind could conceive of one inch equalling a hundred miles.'

Comedian **Ricky Grover** on working with Jo Brand: 'She came on stage and introduced me as her twin brother but compared with her I'm anorexic. Twice round her and I'd be out of petrol.'

Dudley Moore on the Deep South: 'People are incredibly polite. Even their war was civil.'

Terry Hall of The Specials: 'This is it, my little petals, last chance to dance before World War Three.'

Mick Hucknall: 'I fear most what the world fears, AIDS. Not just for my own sake, but for everybody's. If anybody I knew told me they had it but still refused to change their sexual behaviour, I'd thump them.'

Boxer **Terry Marsh**: 'I never touch alcohol, because after two pints I want to fight them.'

Roxanne Shante: 'Now with the crack drug epidemic, it's not safe anymore. People are smoking it night and day and robbing and maiming each other. You can't even trust your best friends now.'

LL Cool J: 'I call myself a rap gangster, but it doesn't mean I waste people and throw them into rivers, I just like the respect that surrounds gangsters.'

Tim Westwood: 'In the summer we're holding an open-air jam on Wormwood Scrubs Common, next to the prison. They'll be raving behind the walls—we've got plenty of home boys inside.'

Rowland Rivron: Knock, knock! Who's there? The Police.'

Perry Fenwick: 'I was turned away from a Dexy's Midnight Runners Night because I was too smart, I wasn't wearing rags and dirt on my face.'

Ray Winstone: 'My dad always said it's no good being poor and looking poor. When I'm skint I've always got a good suit on.'

Redskins: 'Being a skinhead used to mean taking a stand, making things clear. Stop talking about challenge when you challenge nothing.'

On meeting **Barry White**: 'He talks with a voice so deep, only the creatures at the bottom of the ocean can understand him.'

On **Soul II Soul:** 'To think my LWR show once clashed with Jazzie's Kiss show—yet he has my full respect each and every time.'

On **Lenny Henry**: 'Sort that hideous yellow jacket out—you look like a *Hi-de-Hi* entertainer.'

On **Natalie Cole**: 'With that, she slumps deeper into the sofa—thankfully looking more like a Peppermint Lounge suffragette than a photogenic lip-smacking victim.'

After leaving the NME I would say my best interviewee was Johnny Vaughan who, when my batteries ran out at the start, ran around trying to get me replacements in the office. And then proceeded to give me a fabulous two-hour interview despite his manager telling us to finish; Johnny said 'go away, I'm enjoying this'. He then whisked me through the *Big Breakfast* studio to take a photo of me and Denise Van Outen, who I told him I had a bit of a crush on. The worst interviewee was undoubtedly Rupert Everett who in my experience was snobbish and terminally dull.

Colourful quotes were all fine and dandy but at the NME the tide was turning against me. Spencer was to announce he was going and a chap called Ian Pye replaced him. I was about to get in touch with Julie Burchill for the first time for an interview I was commissioned to do for *Just 17*. But I daren't tell Uncle Tone, pugilist of the parish. Julie was living a life straight out of the movie *Sweet Smell of Success* with the bright young things in the Groucho Club.

Tony, meanwhile, moved to Highbury to the appropriately named Poets' Road and found a strange allegiance to Arsenal despite being a lifetime West Ham supporter (my team). He started writing for a soccer fanzine and picked my brain on this; he particularly liked the stuff I told him about West Ham's Inter-City Firm having a calling card that said, 'Congratulations you have just been cut by the ICF'. He was a bit bloodthirsty, old Tone was. After working for *The Face* and the *Telegraph,* he decided to take a column on the *Mirror*. This was the paper his parents had taken all their life and even though he was worried about working for a tabloid, he thought it was a quality tabloid.

9: The NME within

THE meaty, beaty, big and bouncy NME days were best described by my ex-editor Neil Spencer.

PW: What were your initial thoughts on being introduced to me by Tony Parsons as a writer for the NME ?

NS: 'Another cockney chancer looking for a break ... well, if he's any good he can have one.'

PW: Was I the first soccer casual writer on the music press?

NS: Not sure. I think Kevin Sampson, king of the scouse casuals, was already stringing for us from the 'Pool.

PW: What did you think being a good editor of the NME involved?

NS: Great people skills; managing a bunch of gifted but deranged egos. Knowing how to handle IPC and keep them at a distance while making them crazy amounts of money. Knowing whose musical judgement to trust. Recognising good writers in the making, even if they weren't the finished article. Visual flair. Going out and seeing what was going on at ground level (no other editors did). Being aware that popular music exists in a wider cultural context (ditto).

PW: What will be your legacy?

NS: No idea. That's for others to decide.

PW: What were you most proud of and ashamed of?

NS: I took the paper to greater sales than it had since Beatlemania, and which it has never managed since. I filled the paper with vibrant writing and visual talent. I challenged the notion of what a music magazine could be and could achieve. I stood up against the Nazification of rock music,. I shouldn't have let things slip in the middle of my reign. I was having an unhappy time in my personal life, and I don't have the constitution for endless hours in the office. (I've never returned to full-time office employment since I left NME.)

PW: Any other comments on my writing?

NS: I recall your writing as getting there rather than being the finished article. I told every new writer to go and read Orwell's *Politics and the English Language* as a guide on what to do and not to do. As to the rebellion/criminality bit—well, no slur on your politics implied. Chippy yes, but then I didn't mind that. I used to hire middle class kids (Barney, Mat) AND working class kids (Amanda Root, you). I considered myself a working class hero/wannabe. These days I can't think why anyone, including me, would be 'proud to be working class'. We come from where we come from, the important thing is to be who we really are, and that means transcending our background. No reason to feel ashamed or inferior 'cos your parents are working class but then it ain't necessarily a virtue either. But when you're young and growing up in a class-ridden society like Britain, such lofty thoughts are not really what propels us on. As for the criminality, I do recall you being infatuated by the East End gangland thing. In fact, when I saw you after we'd both moved on from the NME you seemed to be even more in love with it. Later still, you'd gotten disaffected with it all.

PW: What do you think of the NME now?

NS: It's struggling to reinvent itself in the wake of Britpop and find its place in the midst of a far more aggressive and complicated and widespread pop coverage. It needs a bandwagon to hitch itself to, and Pop Idol ain't it. The Strokes help, but British pop is in a dreadful state.

PART TWO

1: The *Mirror* cracked

TONY Parsons went to the *Daily Mirror* and Blair was on the campaign trail still pretending to stick to real Labour values. I decided to follow Parsons and renew my faith in journalism—working for the paper under Maxwell and after his unfortunate demise. Although not as horrendously liberal and bourgeois as the NME, the *Mirror* didn't have too many people with proletarian vigour and rebellion. Around this time I became closer to Tony's estranged partner and class warrior, Julie Burchill.

In 1985 she invited me to a party titled 'Fall of the House of Style' at Toby Young's house where she introduced me as the person who was 'the best interviewer she'd had'. She opened the door in black silk stockings, heels and no doubt her favourite Janet Reger underwear and looked like Ava Gardner's more beautiful sister. I was smitten. Conversely, Toby Young irritated me greatly. Then I was introduced to someone who was going to be another hero of mine, style guru Peter York. Peter was one of Julie's closest friends, referring to her as 'the cleverest woman in Britain', something I wholeheartedly agreed with. He was camp, affected, terribly middle class—everything I wasn't—but I loved him. I felt like the character in JD Salinger's *Catcher in the Rye* who dreams of knowing an author so well you can just ring them up and tell them what you thought of their books. I had that with Tony Parsons, now I had it with Julie and Peter. Julie said to me: 'Peter's really going to like you.' To this day I'm so proud to be on Peter York's Christmas card list—as I think he is one of the most astute and perceptive style writers around, and I'm honoured he gave me his last copy of *Style Wars*—one of the funniest book on rebel tribes. Ironically, the last time I met him was watching Tim Fountain's play on Julie Burchill and he was discussing with me whether to bury the hatchet with Toby Young who was reviewing the play for *The Spectator*.

Rebel radio
If you'll allow me a further diversion before I get back to the *Daily Mirror* and Blair, around this time I was involved in some anti-establishment broadcast journalism DJ'ing for LWR (so NOT New Labour), the pirate station that launched Radio 1's Westwood and Pete Tong, with my own mix of mellow two-step R'n'B music. Although not a great DJ, I was good at chatting on the mike and was a genuine musical connoisseur. We

played the rarest grooves from the most dangerous studios in areas like the North Peckham estate and helped launch Soul II Soul to become a mainstream act. Working on rebel radio was a joy.

Pirate radio in the 1980s emerged out of two basic commitments: a belief in the freedom of the airwaves, and a belief in the music. In those early pioneering days the scene was dominated by radio enthusiasts (anoraks) and black music fans (soul heads). The radio pirates shared the same music, language, and behaviour as their audience; through the adverts they shared the same nightclubs, fashions, clothes, even food and cosmetics. Black music pirates had become part of black music culture. Sadly, great music presenters such as Paul 'Trouble' Anderson and Trevor Shakes were replaced by more commercial newcomers such as CJ Carlos and Chris Stewart. A climate of confusion, hardship and conflict started to pervade pirate radio. A station would lose a new secret studio location within hours of broadcasting; one pirate hacksaws a rival's aerial in half; a station owner is assaulted; and internal squabbles create a dozen breakaway groups.

As Tim Westwood said in the great book *Rebel Radio*, 'the biggest threat to pirate radio has always been legal radio. If legal radio were to start playing the right music with the right style of presentation, it would mean the death of the pirates. Will the legal stations get it right? I believe they will.' Westwood went on to get it right on legal Radio 1. But he wasn't always an Ali G soundalike, the son of the Bishop of Peterborough trying to be 'one of the young hip hop big dogs from behind the walls straight outta Compton'; he was a brilliant DJ and journalist. I interviewed him for the *Evening Standard* and toured the country with him in his Ford Escort Estate alongside, on a couple of occasions, the mighty Trevor Nelson (who always looked like Miles Davis *circa* 'A kind of Blue'), and he sneaked myself and 'one of the brothers' from Dalston into a room at the Prestatyn Soul Weekender. I used to stand in the DJ booth with him and learn how to mix, scratch and chat. I also slept round Westood's tiny flat in Hammersmith and it was the most minimalist place I'd ever seen—just his boxes of records and about three books. He was famous then for only ever eating sandwiches, smoking spliff, wearing black, and reverse racism—ie, never going out with white women. In those days he supported radical Public Enemy Hip Hop and played the mellowest R'n'B but now he supports reactionary Gangsta Rap which seems to glamorise violence, homophobia and misogyny. Sad.

My career on pirate radio was another extension of my journalism. But to this day I wonder what makes a group of people defy the law and risk heavy fines all for no pay. The clandestine crew of LWR went from a dingy office in Brixton to a cupboard in Crystal Palace. The station was hidden deep in *Minder* land, broadcasting on 92.5 to listeners as far away as Slough. The station had a pool of 35 DJs, 28 of them regulars, and advertised on air for more; six had daily shows. They had colourful *noms de guerre* like Lone Ranger, Jasper, Jigs and The Wing Commander, and the standard of professionalism varied wildly. But on LWR you had more freedom than on legitimate stations. Music was its politics to 1.5 million listeners. There was an insinuation that if we went legal we would incite London youth to riot—which was crap. The music created our popularity. That and people wanting us to compete. The DJs tried to convince everyone listening that they were the best while they were on. It was the satisfaction of knowing we were number one, of eroding the established stations, of being able to hear LWR anywhere in London and knowing it's something that founders like the energetic Zak created.

I was trying to pioneer alongside Desi Parkes and Paul Anderson before me the 'Two Step' or 'Speng music' scene. A typical Two Step crowd was aged 25 upwards and the music was mid-tempo, often heard in illegal house (rather than warehouse) parties and dingy little clubs with modest décor and poor lighting, such as The People's Club in Paddington. Tunes were often spun by ardent collectors making a precarious living as a DJ. The soul was interspersed with Lovers rock.

Aside from this purist scene there were clubs catering for a younger generation such as Gossips on a Friday (the longest-running soul club in the West End) mixing mellow soul with more upfront hip hop and house. Speng music was usually old American but Rick Clarke was the British face of it. Unfortunately this great British singer never crossed over to mainstream chart success. One of the most popular Two Step anthems was Natalie Cole's 'This Will Be', a guaranteed floor-filler just like Odyssey's 'Don't Tell Me Tell Her'. Around 1984 tracks like Sheree Brown's 'It's a Pleasure' and 80s Ladies' 'Turned on to you' were the underground sound of the seventies getting some revival pressure. Not forgetting Barbara Streisand's 'Guilty' and Ricky Lee Jones 'Chuck E's In Love' for some crossover. Eddie Harris 'It's Allright now' was my radio theme tune and the JBs' 'Same Beat' was moving the crowd. In 1985 Norman Jay's Good Times Sound and Soul II Soul changed their 'two step tunes' for the rare groove seventies sound and in the late eighties we mixed it up with mellow house tunes like Raze's 'Break 4 Love', Izit's 'Stories' and conscious rap such as De La Soul's 'Say No Go'. But DJs like Desi Parkes, whose house in Forest Gate contained one of the best record collections I've ever seen, and Paul Anderson pioneered the seventies sound all along. The Two Step phenomenon is still prevalent today with the sounds of Erykah Badu, Angie Stone, Alicia Keys, Jill Scott and India Arie. Meanwhile, Tony Blair is still listening to his King Crimson albums.

2: Fleet Street in retreat

FLEET Street *was* journalism to me. But the Street of Ink, the middle-priced red one after Free Parking on the Monopoly board that nobody really wants, is finally dead. Long live the Docklands. Reuters, the last major news association left on the street, has decided to up shop and move out to Canary Wharf. Hacksville is no more. The global news and information group announced in September 2003 that it was shifting all of its 3,000 London staff to new 281,000 sq ft headquarters and selling its historic Fleet Street building after 64 years. Formerly home to every major news association in the UK, Fleet Street will soon become a journalism-free zone when Reuters completes its move. Fleet Street, former hang-out of William Shakespeare, Ben Jonson, Samuel Pepys, Mark Twain and Charles Dickens, has played host to the UK's national newspaper industry since 1500, when de Worde, an apprentice of the pioneer of printing, William Caxton (1422-91), set up shop in the area.

John Ezard, writing in *The Guardian*, said that Reuters, the once mega-rich and now troubled agency, was expected to make £32m from the move. Its departure will turn a thronged, narrow road in central London known 100 years ago as the Street of Adventure, and to *Private Eye* more recently as the Street of Shame, into a street of spectres.

Frank Miles, who at 79 was still working at the once-legendary London Press Club, remembers the old press days: 'People did not take proper meal breaks and spent too long in pubs, drinking on empty stomachs. There was this sense of the power of the press and of a great rivalry and camaraderie mixed together—rivals all being in the same pubs together. The press was the Fourth Estate. It smelt of power, and the competition to get stories, which were breaking all the time. It was a wonderful place to be in, a fun place.'

The street's two most dominating press empires were the *Daily Telegraph*'s classical headquarters and the Art Deco building of the *Daily Express* and *Sunday Express*, dubbed 'the black Lubyanka' by *Private Eye*. Mac's Cafe, the printers' and journalists' greasy spoon which never closed, is a Starbucks. The Cheshire Cheese has a plaque commemorating Dr Johnson's completion of the first English dictionary there in 1755. But the pub is empty of hungry hacks for tourists to gaze at.

Frank Miles adds: 'What I have never understood is why they could not introduce new [printing] technology, yet keep the buildings. It is most sad to walk up Fleet Street now. It really is a ghost town.'

My Fleet Street journey was a switchback ride. After a brief spell with London's *Evening Standard*, working alongside Richard Littlejohn, who I thought was a great writer, despite his politics being to the right of Genghis Khan, I had found myself in the Street. I would take long liquid lunches with journos and the printers in true Jeffrey Barnard fashion.

At the *Evening Standard* I worked on Peter Holt's Showbiz Column 'Ad Lib' with the erudite Spencer Bright, the lovely Rosalind Russell and Jane Goldman—Jonathan Ross's wife who was really sweet and asked me to take her to accounts to sort out her expenses. She was one of the most beautiful woman I had ever seen; Jonathan is a very lucky man. I also spoke to the famous film critic Alexander Walker and respected his opinions on the movies greatly, although he didn't seem to share my total passion for the films of Ken Loach.

Being from humble origins, I had never had money and now I was earning bundles of dough. As a shift worker at the end of the day, I was taught how to record imaginary expenses and take it to the accounts department and get £90 a day for my shift plus 'exes' in cash. I blew the lot each day on clothes, drink and records—but what a wonderful world Fleet Street was, I thought.

But then Murdoch moved in and spoilt it for everyone. It was not just high-earning printers who were sacked, in the most violent industrial dispute ever seen on the streets of London, but among the 5,000 axed workers—as Bill Bryson points out in his book *Notes from a Small Island*—were hundreds of lower-paid librarians, clerks, secretaries, cleaners and messengers whose only crime was to have joined a union.

Spencer Bright, author of the amusing best-selling biography *Take It Like a Man—the Boy George Story,* recalls those days far more accurately and eloquently than I could: 'There's always a problem breaking into Fleet Street if you haven't gone the usual routes, whether through the mill via local and regional papers, or, if you have them, family connections or come from the privileged class. The *Standard* of those days was largely peopled by the talented, with a smattering who owed their presence to looking the part.

'The "Ad Lib" desk was a little fiefdom of its own ruled by Old Etonian Peter Holt. He, I'm sure, would now admit he was more interested in the partying possibilities bestowed by the job remit rather than the journalism. Peter is a talented writer but he wasn't a great team leader, probably because essentially he's too nice a chap. His second in command was feisty Scot Rosalind Russell, who had been on now-defunct music paper *Record Mirror.*

'I was there because I too liked having a good time, while at the same time suffering the resentment any member of a diary or column team suffers, that of having no byline recognition. In my case I reckoned I put more than my fair share of work into the column. One thing Peter was very good at was protecting his position, making sure no-one else got too much glory. I was foolishly over-loyal. I was there eight years and in some ways I feel it stunted my advancement as a writer. I believe I only learnt the craft of feature writing after I left there.

'You, Paul, were one of the mavericks we would have in from time to time sitting behind the mound of reference books and papers and giving us some much-needed street cred. Among the people also making an appearance were Emma Freud and Garry Bushell.

'One of Peter's best points was being non-judgemental. So although he couldn't help being upper class and believing in *droit de seigneur* (if you know what I mean), he was open to influences from all spheres. So it was with your natural pugilistic looks and cockney charm. I suppose there might have been an element of 'how quaint these working class chaps are', but it was buried, and I don't believe he treated you with condescension.

'I remember you writing about boxing and black music and having a deep understanding, respect, and—dare I say it—love, for the characters you were portraying, even if they were not necessarily that savoury. You were proud of your background and I sensed you felt that a lot of life in London was not being adequately covered or reflected in the *Evening Standard*. Your standards of prose writing were high and you demanded the best of yourself. It was clear you had a love of words, and a knowledge of their power, and were open to the rhythms and vernacular of the street. In some ways the "Ad Lib" column, having essentially a flippant tone, was not the right place for your style of writing. I felt you should have been given more scope to write features. I believe the features you wrote were well received, but it was often difficult getting the features desk to understand we needed more of this type of writing.

'Those were the days before the *Standard* made a conscious effort to be hip. It was just before the explosion of the club scene with the coming of Acid House, and before the word 'style' and all deeds in its name were elevated to the level of holy writ. After that it was a plus to be as superficial as possible. It was at this point that I left to pursue writing books and journalism with a wider palette.

'Richard Littlejohn was always a great character on the *Standard*. I remember him as industrial correspondent. He was always highly competent and definitely one of the lads, who could pack the pints away. I was never one of them. However, I was always a kind of a mate with Richard and on a personal level always found him a warm and generous person, much belying the public image of him as a thug. He began as a columnist on the *Standard* where they recognised his talent for a knockabout comment or two. I may not share his political views—oddly enough, he was a strong union man and always appeared to be on the left—but I've always respected his iconoclasm. We need more like him.

'Garry Bushell I never warmed to. Whereas as a true cockney—yes, I was born within the sound of the Bow Bells—I could understand where Richard was coming from, I couldn't quite gauge Garry. Initially I believe he had quite far-left credentials. But with the advent of the Oi so-called movement in the seventies and its skinhead imagery he began to appear to stand for something quite distasteful.'

The *Daily Mirror* was never distasteful. Our most enlightened historian AJP Taylor once said: 'The *Daily Mirror* gave an indication as never before of what ordinary people were thinking. The English people at last found their voice.' I had taken the *Mirror* from 1977 and proudly still take it to this day. This was the paper that produced arguably the best journalists ever on the Street of Ink: John Pilger, Paul Foot, Keith Waterhouse, Marj Proops, Paul Routledge and latterly Brian Reade.

I had always believed that the philosophy of the *Mirror* seemed to be compassionate and that every letter, every phone call, was taken deadly seriously. My views would not change radically working both pre- and post- Maxwell at Holborn Circus and at Canary Wharf.

3: Ethical journalism

ETHICS in journalism were important. I wanted to be that rarest of creatures—a journalist with a mass audience and a clear radical commitment. I had a great respect for the power of the written word to intervene—to right injustice, to expose corruption and to puncture the smug hypocrisy of a self-righteous, conspiratorial elite (this was pre-New Labour). Journalists like Greg Palast, Paul Foot and John Pilger are the uncomfortable conscience that will not go away. That is what campaigning journalism is all about or, as Mark Thomas would put it in more intellectual terms, their work was 'fucking brilliant. Just fucking brilliant.'

Journalists are fairly sceptical about the value of a debate on Ethics. 'Effics! It's a county where girls wear their knickers as ankle warmers' comes the liberated response of the neanderthal tabloid hack. As *Financial Times* reporter Raymond Snoddy once said, 'It certainly sets the British press apart from newspapers in the US where on the whole the word "ethics" can be uttered without hoots of derision' (*The Good, the Bad and the Unacceptable,* Faber and Faber').

In an interview with award-winning *Observer* journalist Palast (the man who exposed Blair's underhand tactics and to its shame got called 'The Liar' on the front page of the *Mirror*) I uncovered the following about journalistic ethics.

PW: What do you think of the state of journalism in the UK?

GP: Compared to America, this is journalism's Garden of Eden: I've been able to print stories—from the 'Theft of the US Election by the Bushmen' to an exposé of the dark heart of the World Bank. But since this is my chance to shoot wildly at all moving objects, I'm still stunned that UK journalists put up with the vile libel laws—the privatisation of censorship—a weapon of corporate conmen and killers, and no protector of the truth. Simply the fear of libel action, as opposed to a suit, kills one hell of a lot of investigative reporting. It wouldn't stand up for one minute if the papers took joint action—nor would the villainous Official Secrets Act. In the US, the last vestige of official secrets came to an end when 30 papers simultaneously printed the Pentagon Papers: jail one, jail all; sue one, sue all. That was American journalism's finest hour—30 years ago—unfortunately, its last.

PW: What code of ethics should journalists subscribe to?

GP: Uh, oh: this is an invitation to cliché-ville. Nevertheless, I have to say: don't eat shit. Journalists should take the following pledge each day: 'I will not write from a press release. In fact, I won't read them. I will not attend a press conference. I will not call the same arseholes for the same damn soundbites.'

PW: What do you feel about the *Mirror* returning to its roots and re-employing greats like John Pilger and Paul Foot?

GP: The *Mirror* remains a piece of shit. A marketing decision to piss on Blair after years of sucking his bum does not change its fecal content. Left propaganda is as tiresome as Right propaganda, even if I'm more sympathetic to one over the other. Pilger and Foot are giants—and they are writing provocative and valuable commentaries and opinion pieces. This should not be confused with the *Mirror* providing any information or reporting: unless North London has moved to Kabul.

PW: What do you think of Julie Burchill, Tony Parsons, Danny Baker or Garry Bushell?

GP: I'd like to marry her. So would my wife. It's easy to shoot at Burchill, but I can't get enough of her anger over the slights against the working class. (Note: As an investigative reporter, I do my best to avoid reading newspapers or watching television—so I don't know the rest.)

PW: Who are your favourite journalists and why?

GP: Besides Pilger and Foot, add (in no special order) Robin Ramsey of *Lobster*, Stephen Kerr of the University of Toronto student newspaper, Antony Barnett and Martin Bright of the *Observer,* Solomon Hughes (freelance, sometimes *Red Pepper*), Finnegan Wa Simbeye of *Tanzanian Guardian*, John Nichols and David Corn (*Nation*), Danny Schechter (MediaChannel.org), and many others I'm ashamed to forget as I'm typing away.

PW: What qualities constitute a good journalist to you?

GP: Someone who hunts for the information that the powers-that-be would keep hidden: that's news. Someone willing to take the time to get to the core documents that underlie the story and understand them. Larry Ellott wrote: 'Palast thinks investigative journalism is the only journalism; the rest is PR.' Amen.

PW: What is your funniest/most embarrassing moment in journalism?

GP: Read Chapter 7, 'Lobbygate', of my book *The Best Democracy Money Can Buy.*

PW: What are you most proud of?

GP: Before I was a journalist I had a real job: heading racketeering investigations. My two most important: putting a rotten nuclear plant builder out of business and uncovering, for the Chugach Natives of Alaska, the frauds that led to the Exxon Valdez disaster.

* * * *

In the pursuit of muck-raking exposés, my first visit to the *Daily Mirror* was at its former Holborn headquarters in 1979 to interview my favourite journalist of the time, columnist Paul Foot—an investigative reporter of the year. He told me that when a journalist from a rival paper taunted him with the line 'I admire your writing but have no brief for your schoolboy socialism', he replied that it was his deeply-held socialist beliefs that made his writing what it was. Foot sadly suffered from the jibe that his background was more SW1 than his beloved SWP.

After going to the Newspaper Library in Colindale, North London, I had found that during the Second World War the Daily Mirror Readers' Service was set up to support families while the main earner was away at war. Anybody could use the Readers' Service, which got 'justice' from the system for countless thousands of powerless people: the elderly, disabled people, single parents, people in need of legal advice. It was entirely free and what the *Mirror* got in return was a loyal readership. The *Mirror* was the first popular paper to encourage working class people to express themselves, and this was their newspaper to do it in. When someone came to reception and asked to see the editor, it was assumed that a reporter would be sent down to help, regardless of whether a story was being offered.

There was a code of ethics drafted long before the NUJ (National Union of Journalists) wrote one. Staff were made aware that if they knowingly submitted false or distorted stories, they would be out on their ear. The same applied to 'foot-in-the-door' and similar harassment against ordinary people, although this did not apply to seeking information from the privileged and the criminal.

This was a paper you were proud to work for. I remember reading in the archives the columnist Cassandra (William Connor) describing the 'silent tragedy' facing old people. 'As science grapples successfully with the enemy of early death,' he wrote, 'a paradoxical blight of new unhappiness descends. Life, propped up by new skills, resurrected by new medical research and by new drugs, finds new and implacable enemies. You come to a point where all your contemporaries, good or bad, are your friends [because] poverty is often your last companion. When [the writer] O'Henry lay dying, he was credited with saying, "Turn up the light, I am afraid to go home in the dark." For those who will help, there is still time to rescue the aged before it is dark.'

4: The *Mirror*—a history

AS the 2003 centenary edition of the *Mirror* will tell you:

One hundred years ago this year the Daily Mirror *was born. A century in which the* Mirror *became the people's champion.*

This is the newspaper which shocked the Establishment in 1910 by printing a front-page picture of Edward VII on his deathbed.

This is the newspaper Churchill tried to get banned during the Second World War. And which ever since has left pompous ministers choking over their muesli.

The Daily Mirror *has backed the Labour Party since the mid-thirties The* Mirror *was the first newspaper for the working man and woman.*

It was born at a time when women didn't have the vote and working class people were treated as second-class citizens or worse.

The Labour Party, created three years earlier, gave them a political body. The Daily Mirror *gave them a true voice.*

The ruling class used to believe (and some elements still believe) it could dictate to the people and they would do what their masters told them. They were there as voting fodder at elections and cannon fodder in wartime. It was very upstairs downstairs.

The Mirror *was not prepared to accept that line. Run by people like Hugh Cudlipp and Harry Guy Bartholomew who believed in everyone's right to know, it confronted every bit of the Establishment.*

The Mirror *ran a fabulous post-war election campaign urging voters to back Labour against Churchill for the sake of peace.*

That led not just to victory but to the historic Labour government which founded the health service and created the modern welfare state.

They initially saw in Tony Blair a leader who could put Labour back into power and were his loudest cheerleaders.

Its biggest disagreement with Tony Blair has been over the war in Iraq.

The Mirror *has never been an anti-war paper on principle. There are times when war is necessary and as a nation and a newspaper they have never shirked from that.*

But the Mirror *has always opposed unjust wars. It attacked the conflicts in Vietnam and Suez, and was proved right in both cases. And so the* Mirror *enters its second century. Still fighting for what it believes is right and still willing to upset the Establishment.*

Even Tony Blair paid tribute to the *Mirror* through gritted teeth: 'The *Daily Mirror* has informed, educated and entertained the British people through a century of enormous change and challenge. Never afraid to make waves, never afraid to stand up for its readers, the paper has been the home of some of this country's finest journalists and journalism. The *Mirror* has also been a staunch supporter of the Labour Party even in our bleakest days.

'We don't, of course, always agree. But our enduring bond rests on the shared and decent values of our party and *Mirror* readers and on our common determination to build a better, fairer society for all.

'Congratulations to the *Mirror* and its readers on this very special anniversary and my best wishes for the next 100 years.'

Like *The Guardian*'s Roy Greenslade, I've had a love affair with the *Daily Mirror* for many years. I first saw the paper in the late 1970s. I was just one of its millions of readers, an ordinary teenager who first picked it up simply because it was delivered to our house. I remember John Pilger's report from Cambodia and being genuinely scared by it.

The *Mirror* spoke my kind of language—direct, punchy and informative. The real reason for its circulation explosion in the 1950s was its empathy with the people who had fought and suffered during the war. It was absolutely the forces' favourite. It was, like the Labour Party and the trades unions, on 'our' side against 'them'—the have-nots against the haves. Much was expected of the incoming Labour government by the *Mirror* and its readers and it still is. The *Mirror*'s sale went above 5m for the first time in 1964, the year Harold Wilson came to power, and rose to more than 5.2m just after the 1966 election.

The gradual movement away from the *Mirror* to the *Sun* from 1970 onwards wasn't political at first, but the *Sun* had a simple advantage: it caught the spirit of the time, breaking with Labour at the time of people's greatest disillusion and supporting the baby-boomers' materialism. Despite all that, the *Mirror* still retains 2m buyers, and there is life in the underdog yet.

Tracing the history in more detail, the highs and lows of the paper were many. In 1903 Alfred Harmsworth launched the *Daily Mirror* as a 'paper for gentlewomen'. Hamilton Fyfe took over within a year, changing the emphasis to photo-journalism. In 1915 the *Sunday Pictorial* was launched as a photo-journal (renamed the *Sunday Mirror* in 1963).

In 1914, Northcliffe offloaded his shares in the *Mirror* to his brother, Lord Rothermere, who controlled it until he sold the majority of his interest in 1931. Lord Rothermere went on to poison his *Daily Mail* with his fascism, with the unbelievable front page splash 'Hoorah for the Blackshirts', while leaving the *Mirror* without an owner. Although Rothermere's chairman, John Cowley, remained in charge, on the board was Cecil Harmsworth King, Rothermere's nephew and an unusual aristocrat.

As advertising director, King set off changes on the *Mirror* that turned it into a campaigning 'paper of the Left', as the *Mirror* was to rebrand itself. He changed the *Daily Mirror* into the first modern tabloid. But it was Hugh Cudlipp, a boy from the Welsh Valleys, who would eventually reposition the *Mirror* as a paper of its times. In 1935 he joined as assistant features editor before moving to the Sunday paper. Politically, Cudlipp was a true maverick. He believed that popular journalism should reflect the 'decency of ordinary folk', as he put it.

By 1938 he was editor and circulation rose to 1.7m. Later he became director of the Daily Mirror Newspapers Group. In 1953 on Coronation day the *Daily Mirror* broke all world records by selling 7m copies. In 1984 Pergamon Holdings Ltd, owned by Robert Maxwell, bought Mirror Group Newspapers. Later, it was discovered he had plundered the group's pension fund.

In 1994 the Mirror Group left Fleet Street for Canary Wharf and in 1995 Piers Morgan, at 30, became the youngest editor of a national daily newspaper when he left the *News of the World* for the *Daily Mirror*.

With the arrival of Murdoch's *Sun*, dumbing-down of popular journalism had begun. As an American journalist working on one of Rupert's titles said, 'no self-respecting fish would be wrapped in a Murdoch newspaper'. In hindsight, what is astonishing is that the *Mirror* was able to retain so much of its former self. Some of its most powerful Shock Issues were published in the 1970s and early 1980s: 'Divided Britain' on class, 'This Green and Poisoned Land' on the environment. The Thalidomide campaign was pursued for five years by the *Mirror,* seeking justice for working class children damaged by the drug who had been left out of the original cash settlement because mothers or doctors had mislaid the prescription.

During the late 1970s, a group of more than a hundred health consultants secretly supplied the *Mirror* with the first evidence of the human cost of government cuts to the NHS. 'THIS HOSPITAL IS DYING' read the banner headline over a disturbing picture of a closed children's ward.

In 1978, the *Sun*'s circulation finally overtook the *Mirror*'s. In 1979, only the *Mirror* would have the heart to devote eleven pages to events in a far-away country, Cambodia. Every single copy was sold. *Mirror* readers sent more than £500,000 for Pol Pot's victims, most of it in small amounts, including entire pay packets and pensions. The first relief flight was funded solely by them.

John Pilger, in his uplifting book *Hidden Agendas,* noted: 'In the same year, the *Mirror* took on to the staff a journalist who, alone at times, distinguished the paper during some of its most difficult times—Paul Foot.'

Foot told me: 'I was overjoyed, and very nervous, the day I was shown up to this little office on the fourth floor. All I had was a telephone; I didn't even have a telephone directory and had a job getting one. I sat there the whole afternoon thinking this can't be true. No one told me what I had to write ... I had this idea of making millions of ordinary people informants, of establishing a network of readers who felt they could trust me.

'There was a continuous discussion about what should appear in the paper and what shouldn't. There was an instinctive solidarity with the poor and the dispossessed. As a socialist, I had started basically hostile to the capitalist press, but found the *Mirror* a place where all the things that I wanted to do as a journalist—finding things out, challenging the powerful, tackling the government—were possible.'

In 1980, I remember meeting Foot for our interview and he told me about his latest campaign. He had received a letter from Ann Whelan, mother of Michael Hickey, one of four men accused of murdering a thirteen-year-old newspaper boy, Carl Bridgewater. Foot went on to report critical evidence that the confession of one of the four, Patrick Molloy, was beaten out of him and was false, and that the others were also innocent. In 1997, thanks to him, Ann Whelan and others, the men were finally released by the Court of Appeal.

In 1982, at the height of the Falklands War, Foot was shown documents which confirmed that the Peruvian government had brokered a peace agreement between Britain and Argentina. On the day the ambassadors of both countries were due to sign it, a British submarine sank the Argentine cruiser *Belgrano*—on the orders of Prime Minister Thatcher. Foot's investigations showed how far Thatcher would go to continue the war, regardless of the willingness of the Argentinians to compromise. He also reported that her government had been arming the Argentine junta.

The coverage of the Falklands War was one of the last really high points at the *Mirror* until at least 2001. Meanwhile, at the *Sun*, a new more slavering dog was straining at the leash as editor—Kelvin MacKenzie. I met MacKenzie once when I interviewed him for a Channel 4 programme I was doing on the 'dumbing-down of journalism'. He was charming enough but seemed full of sub-Jim Davidson jokes and appeared incredibly arrogant.

Peter Chippendale and Chris Horrie, in their book *Stick It Up Your Punter,* said: 'MacKenzie was a social diver rather than a social climber, playing to the gallery of the rougher end and absorbing the code of the cocky, macho soccer fan personified by Millwall, the club he purported to support.' He of course thought the sinking of the Belgrano which took 1,200 lives merited a one word headline: 'Gotcha!' It was quite amusing to see him recently coming over all compassionate, sensitive and shocked at the tantrums and irrational anger of Naomi Campbell in a recent TV documentary—when in my experience he was far from the shrinking violet himself.

The *Mirror* called the *Sun* 'THE HARLOT OF FLEET STREET'. 'There have been lying newspapers before,' it said, 'but in the past month [the *Sun*] has broken all records. From behind the safety of its typewriters it has called for battle to commence to satisfy its bloodlust. The *Sun* today is to journalism what Dr Joseph Goebbels was to truth.'

During 1982 the *Mirror's* circulation rose slightly and the *Sun's* fell, although the *Sun* remained ahead. Perhaps the arrival of Robert Maxwell was inevitable. He and Rupert Murdoch exemplified the Thatcher years. Between them, they started the decline in popular journalism. I loathed the *Sun* (which strangely has become more inclusive and liberal in the last two years) not because it was so dishonest but because it was so effective. When Murdoch sacked 5,000 News International workers, I used to live around the corner from the dispute in Wapping and hear the strikers' black humour.

I also infiltrated News International undercover as a refuse collector but never got to write a story. However, I once had to empty the then *Sunday Times* editor Andrew Neil's bin at his office and saw him look down his nose at me as if I was something he'd trodden in at a cattle market. Meanwhile, Maxwell was to reduce the *Mirror's* circulation and campaigning journalism. Even one of my favourite editors, Richard Stott, became a Maxwell apologist; the headline 'THE MAN WHO SAVED THE *MIRROR*' was splashed across the front page the day after the great fraudster's death in November 1991.

I only met the 'Fat Controller' once, when he was in reception, saying he would shun lifts and only eat in the office canteen, not something I ever saw him do. 'Who are you?' he bellowed. 'Paul Wellings—doing shifts for the *Mirror* Showbiz team,' I answered. 'Any good?' he replied. 'I think so,' I said. 'Good, keep up the good work,' he stated in his patronising, autocratic manner.

Maxwell, despite Joe Haines (Harold Wilson's former press officer) warning people about this very fact, went on to rob *Mirror* pensioners and alienate core *Mirror* readers such as the miners, dockers and unemployed with his Thatcherite editorial, which he actually changed himself many times before the paper was put to bed—much to many writers' dismay.

Although I did file some serious social-conscience stories that stood up, I also supplemented my income with some funnies. I had made a friendship with a guy I met at *Sounds* called Garry Johnson, who is one of the funniest people I'd ever encountered. Johnson was a cockney boy who grew up in Essex (and as you may know there are more East Enders in Essex and Hertfordshire than in the East End) but was a big supporter of Derek Hatton and Militant. His attitude to life was 'never take anything seriously' and we didn't, making up stories about someone 'selling David Bowie air (as breathed by the great man himself) in jars outside a concert'. The *Mirror* knew it was a fun story and printed it and paid us. I'm sure the *Mirror* readers knew it was a made-up, fun story as well—so there was no conflict with ethical truthfulness. Initially I did shifts for John Blake on the *Mirror* (now a successful publisher) in Showbiz and saw the confrontational, aggressive style of Anne 'Weakest Link' Robinson at first hand. The columnist fell under the Maxwell spell and described his 'sense of daring and fearlessness that was truly astounding. He was, in truth, part monster, part magic ... He enriched many lives. Mine was one of them.'

I also became familiar with the 'Tourette's Syndrome' language of Alastair Campbell (the political editor), who would become the most powerful media person in the country. I remember, too, being present with the great Keith Waterhouse doing his own version of *Jeffrey Barnard is Unwell* at the *Mirror*'s local, the White Swan (also known as the Stab in the Back).

Showbiz journalism was all about eating and drinking against the system—there were many weeks when I never paid for food and drink by just going to parties. But after a month of that, you stop going because the same boozers, losers and jacuzzi users were there every night. I also worked alongside Jane Moore who despite her more conservative politics was a delightful colleague, even making me coffees (a rarity among Fleet Street journos). The biggest gap at the *Mirror* to this day is radical women writers.

One of the funniest people there was Nick Ferrari (now a radio shock-jock and proposed editor of the new London *Evening Mail*) who despite being a rabid right-winger made me laugh uncontrollably with his 'Smashy and Nicey' impressions. He said to me, 'Wellings, you're not going to swing a chainsaw at me, are you?' as I had apparently threatened him in a drunken stupor in the dim and dark past.

Another bizarre chapter in the *Mirror* story came when Roy Greenslade, now a media commentator for *The Guardian*, started a smear campaign against Arthur Scargill and his supposed links with President Quadhafi. This was proved to be patently untrue. *The Guardian*'s Seamus Milne was the only investigative reporter to say Scargill had been set up. Milne wrote in a postscript to his book *The Enemy Within*: 'The British mining industry is now privatised, most of it sold to Richard Budge, a man identified in a confidential 1994 report for the Trade and Industry Department by the accountants Coopers & Lybrand as "unfit to be concerned in the management of a company". The same was said by the DTI inspectors in 1971 about Robert Maxwell.'

When Maxwell drowned, the *Mirror* devoted eleven pages of sycophancy to this ruthless man. An editorial called him 'The giant with a vision ... under him our commitment to social justice and political decency was strengthened.' I'm sure the *Mirror* pensioners were pleased to read that. It got worse: 'MAXWELL: £526 *MILLION* IS MISSING' the paper would eventually say. The money, said the *Mirror,* had 'vanished' in the week before Maxwell died and it 'includes £526 *million* from the pension fund'. Maxwell had stolen this fortune from the *Mirror's* pensioners, including those who had devoted their working lives to the paper.

5: The *Mirror* today

TODAY'S *Mirror* is produced at Canary Wharf, the landmark building in London's Docklands. Ironically it is just along the river from Murdoch's Fortress Wapping. The *Mirror* offices occupy the top floors. I worked under David Banks here as editor, who was quite prepared to let me talk in his office and phone him late to tell him I was proud to work for the *Mirror* as my parents were both Labour voters, and he said: 'I'm extremely pleased to hear that.' In a cynical hack world, he was a compassionate man and I never once doubted his sincerity. He was a genuine socialist who had his hands tied by managers like David Montgomery. The current *Mirror* editor, Piers Morgan, gave me some freelance work and once showed me around Fortress Wapping when he was showbiz editor of the *Sun*.

Morgan made his name running the *Sun*'s 'Bizarre' column and having his photograph taken with 'celebrities'. Thereafter he was appointed editor of the *News of the World* at the tender age of twenty-eight, the youngest editor of a national newspaper for fifty years. His other claim to infamy is that he is the only Murdoch editor to have been publicly rebuked by the proprietor about journalistic standards. He was said to have 'gone too far' in publishing photographs of 'anorexic' Countess Spencer, the sister-in-law of the Princess of Wales.

Morgan's guru at Canary Wharf was Kelvin MacKenzie, his old editor at the *Sun* and Murdoch's 'favourite editor'. MacKenzie had joined the Mirror Group as the managing director of the ill-fated cable television company, L!ve TV, which introduced the 'News Bunny' to broadcasting. 'News Bunny', a person dressed in a rabbit costume, sat beside the newscaster and commented on the news of the day giving a dumb thumbs-up or down to the news. Janet Street Porter famously stood up to him in the excellent documentary *Trouble at the Top* and MacKenzie hit back in his usual macho style by saying when Janet was made editor of *The Independent on Sunday* 'she couldn't edit a bus ticket'. In 1998, he was, scarily, appointed managing director of all the company's newspapers.

David Montgomery shares Murdoch's reactionary world view, particularly his aversion to trade unions. His mission at the *Mirror* has been solely to make a profit. He started by sacking 100 journalists, turned away when they arrived for work. He then turned on the NUJ, whose chapel officials were told they must resign or be sacked. They decided to go.

For the first time in the *Mirror*'s history, its journalists passed a vote of no-confidence in its editor, the Montgomery-appointed but left-leaning David Banks. After fourteen years, Paul Foot went, though not before he had devoted his last, unpublished column to the *Mirror* disaster and distributed it on the steps of the old *Mirror* building in Holborn Circus. I remember picking up a copy. More union people and the entire security staff, including a number of *Mirror* veterans, were told to leave the building immediately. As they went, replacements from a low-wage private company arrived. They had been waiting outside in a van. It was almost like another Murdoch coup.

This did not stop the *Mirror* from declaring itself 'The paper that fights for a fairer Britain'. A series of articles claiming to 'speak up for the rights of part-timers' was blessed by the TUC general-secretary, John Monks, who conveniently didn't mention the many part-timers Montgomery had sacked. Similarly, a 'Rolling Rose' recruitment drive by the Labour Party was launched in the *Mirror* by the deputy leader, John Prescott, without referring to the sackings. New party members received the *Mirror* free for a week and drew lots for the privilege of taking tea with Tony Blair. In 1996, Blair called for an easing of the legal limits on the ambitions of newspaper companies to buy into television, which would benefit both the Mirror Group and Murdoch. All the papers (bar the *Mail* and the *Telegraph*) were backing the New Labour project. It was now Blair's media. The most right-wing Labour leader ever now had the media where he wanted them.

Perhaps the most important loss at this time was the *Mirror*'s coverage of politics. *Mirror* editorials had none of the power, knowledge and dry wit of former leader writers. The paper's backing for New Labour became slavish. Blair's speech to the conference was described as 'Labour coming home' when the truth was that he had abandoned the party's traditional beliefs just like the *Mirror* was deserting its traditional readers.

It went from the sublime to the downright silly. When the *Mirror* was handed the political scoop of the year after the Budget papers were leaked to it, Morgan bizarrely handed these back to the government, then published 'tributes' from the establishment for his 'act of responsibility'. At a stroke, the *Mirror*'s proudest tradition of investigative journalism was destroyed and the British secret state had enlisted a new bed fellow. The veteran freelance journalist Peter Hounman, whose hard work had caused the 'leak', was never consulted.

On the day England played Germany at football in the Euro '96 competition, Morgan had published a front page which said, 'ACHTUNG! SURRENDER' as a joke in a bid to get the youth vote. The majority of *Mirror* readers were over 65 and Morgan was desperate for the 'Yoof'.

Except that the youth seemed to think the paper insulted their intelligence. The wanted more campaigns. But the campaigns were few and far between.

Another saw the *Mirror*'s front page dominated by a man's face morphed into that of a pig. This was based on Tim Holley, chief executive of Camelot, which runs the National Lottery. In the graphics mouth was a wad of cash. The headline said: 'LICENSED TO SWILL'. In the news story the pig becomes a 'fat cat' for paying himself the sum of £725,000 including bonuses. One fat cat was left out. David Montgomery, the then chief executive of the Mirror Group, who cashed in shares worth £2.4m.

In 1997, the *Daily Mirror* was 'relaunched' for £16m, although how this money was spent remains a bit of a mystery. The traditional 'Daily' was dropped from the masthead and replaced by 'The *Mirror* ... *The paper for the new millennium'.* It looked like a throwaway 'free sheet'. Pin-ups were now on the front page. Morgan announced that the *Mirror* would be distinct from the 'misogynist' *Sun,* but it didn't seem to be that different. The appointment in 1998 of Kelvin MacKenzie as editor-in-chief because 'the tabloids have gone too downmarket' must have been a joke too far. Circulation was down and soon the mass-market *Mirror* was overtaken, frighteningly, by the housewives' choice, the middle-market *Daily Mail* which wanted to take everyone back to the 1950s.

John Pilger wrote in his book *Hidden Agendas:* 'The question arises: could a mass-circulation *Mirror,* restored to its former glory, succeed today? Probably not: too much has changed. But that is not to say that a bold, quality tabloid, with the same values as the old *Mirror* and a radical mind of its own, could not take the so-called middle ground by storm, challenging the supremacy of the *Daily Mail.* Such a paper, I believe, could prosper if it broke from the present sameness and cynicism that pervade the British press and spoke, once again, as a true agent of people.' How right he was going to be proved, as Piers Morgan took exactly that course of action.

In a recent interview with me, Paul Foot maintained: 'I don't think the *Mirror* is going back to its roots and re-employing people like John Pilger and me as a marketing ploy—I think they are genuinely short of principled journalists.' His best advice to a journalist: 'never be pompous or complacent.'

6: Tony, Julie and me

I WAS to bump into the *Mirror's* Tony Parsons again in 2001 at a media book-reading at London's Festival Hall for his novel, *One For My Baby,* when I asked a question from the floor. I said: 'Glad you're a big success, Tony—I'm here to support you tonight. You recently said in *The Guardian* that you're a right-wing maniac, xenophobic, materialistic, very New Labour, which sounds to me as tolerant as the next guy as long as the next guy is Alf Garnett. You very kindly gave me a break on the NME and were best man at my wedding—but I always remember you as a good socialist—why the change of heart?' To which he replied he'd never been a socialist; he seemed to have selective memory.

He later bounded over to me after the reading and warmly shook my hand and said he'd ring me for lunch. But the call never came. I even tried to get Piers Morgan to reconcile us for lunch but to no avail. Still, I suppose we move on. It is time to let it go. All good things come to an end. I certainly do not want to become some micro-celebrity stalker like Avid Merrion in *Bo Selecta*. Julie Burchill once told me she thought Tony was a 'self-obsessed, idiot prat'. I wouldn't say that, as I will always have a soft spot for Tony (no, not Hackney Marsh).

Once I wanted to be Tony. Now I don't really recognise the friend in wedding photos around our family house and, when my children ask 'who's that, Daddy?', I say 'my friend Tony—I don't see him any more.' But after reading his features about 'dying his hair sun-kissed honey' and eulogising the Queen Mum and Bush's war-mongering, I don't recognise the man. I have nothing in common with him now. I suppose friendship is just people who tell you all the nice things you already knew about yourself anyway.

Tony's views on losing friends can be best explained in the following passage from *One For My Baby*: 'It's not their fault. It's mine. Somehow I have let them all wander off. I do not return their phone calls. I make lame excuses when I receive their invitations to dinner. I do not make the effort, the endless effort, that you need to keep a friendship alive. These are good people. But the truth is that I just don't care enough for the continual contact that friendship demands.' Years ago, I was sure my friends would remain with me until the end; these days I am less convinced. I can only think of two who I am certain will always be there. As Morrissey might have wailed, 'We hate it when our friends become successful but we love it when they fuck up.'

Nowadays my role models are a bit different—genuinely radical people such as Mark Thomas, Mark Steel, Mark Lamarr (in fact anyone called Mark) or Burchill, Pilger, and Foot—the usual suspects. But as the great writer and human rights activist Maya Angelou said, 'Bitterness is like cancer. It eats upon the host. But anger is like fire. It burns all clean.' I've been through my angry young man phase and am now in my compassionate family phase. You get older and mellower. As LP Hartley's novel *The Go Between* says, 'The past is a foreign country. They do things differently there.'

Although my friends from those days are too nice to tell me, I was probably a bit of an asshole in the eighties and had a lot of 'whup ass' attitude—but in the words of *Scarface's* Tony Montana, 'I never fucked anyone over who didn't have it coming to them.'

On the unofficial web site dedicated to Julie Burchill is an accurate picture of the woman: 'b July 1959 in Bristol, joins NME as a "hip young gun-slinger" in 1976; worked for most of the major English press including *The Spectator, Daily Mail, Sunday Times*; fellow hip young gun-slinger (former BBC *Late Review* regular) Tony Parsons and had one son; married another less-hip journo, Cosmo Landesman, and had another son; founding editor *of The Modern Review;* wrote various such as the 1980s-defining blockbuster novel *Ambition,* also *No Exit* and the autobiography *I Knew I was Right.* Formerly the queen of the Groucho Club and possibly the only existent tubby lipstick'd feminist communist, Julie currently writes a weekly column in *The Guardian* and lives a "lotus-eating shopping-and-fucking, self-starting life" in Brighton. Always ironic, surprising and witty yet still managing to be charming, down-to-earth wickedly happy and bright. She has been voted 86th worst Briton.'

In correspondence Julie started to refer to Tony as our 'mutual ex' She wrote: 'I was a card-carrying communist in the late seventies, early eighties when I lived in Billericay funnily enough. I know the idea of a Billericay Communist Party is a bit surreal. But it seemed a perfectly sensible reaction to a mad situation. I think the Communist Party are/were the best of people, except now they've changed their name to something that sounds like a condom. Images? Relate? It was a classic, "The Communist Party of Great Britain", like Coke—you shouldn't muck about with such unique positioning. The best political book I have ever read is *BACKLASH* by Susan Faludi and the best political magazine is *The Modern Review.* My political heroes are Jack Ashley, Cartland and hundreds I don't know the names of. I'd love to see you all this summer. Tell your wife a really hot curry often does the job for a late baby. Love from your incorrigible old chum, Julie.'

That old chum sent me numerous postcards (maybe I'll do an exhibition one day) some with seascapes of Brighton and others such as Max Ernst's unsettling portrait *Triumph des Surrealismus;* a picture of a cat getting the vivisection treatment with the immortal words of Mark Twain, 'Man is the only animal that blushes or needs to'; or fifties-style Beacon book cover cards such as one saying, 'man or woman, sister or brother, her lust knew no bounds'. These cards were typical Julie and said more about her personality than a thousand unauthorised biographies. Just like the unofficial tour of Brighton she gave me the second time I interviewed her for *Mojo* magazine, when she took me to the alley where Phil Daniels shagged Leslie Ash in the exemplary Brit flick *Quadrophenia*.

Another one of her postcards said, "It was *excellent* to see you again and hope you will nip down with your wife and baby when it's really hot. You can all come round and use the pool. Best always.'

And another: 'Just got back from Nassau. It was bloody nice. Hope Lisa and Eve are well and have more news of new magazine that might be good source of work for you called *GEAR* by Bob Guccione JNR (not the porn one, his son). I'll be there. Will be in touch.'

She was even modest about appearing in this book: 'Look at Amis and Rushdie—they've had far more scandalous and eventful lives, and they have international reputations, but no one writes books about them. Tony and I are big fish in a very small pond.' All very well, Julie, but Amis and Rushdie didn't snort speed off the editor's desk and were not the most important part of UK pop journalism.

In her latest interview with me for this book, she said she was no nostalgia freak on the Tony and Julie story: 'I have no interest in Tony apart from him inspiring the odd brilliant catty put-down, which can be heard to effect in the play about me, *JULIE BURCHILL IS AWAY*. I refer you to what I have written about him in the past.'

On the music press: 'When I was working for the music press, obviously I thought I was the best thing on it. Occasionally I buy the NME for my 16-year-old son, and I can barely believe how bland and boring it is. But then I'm 42—it's not MEANT to appeal to me.'

How working class writers are sidelined: 'Working class people have next to no chance of becoming professional writers. And it's getting worse.'

On the TV adaptation of *Man and Boy*: 'I began to watch it, but turned it off when I started to laugh.'

On the book *Man and Boy:* "I've said it before—Gina is slender, decent and dull, so that rules me out. And Harry has all his own hair, is attractive to young women and good in bed. So that rules Tony out.'

On her 'memorable' interviews with me: 'Nothing personal, but I don't remember you interviewing me the first time, and only minimally the second time. I don't have a good memory, and subscribe to Ingrid Bergman's recommendation of what gives the best chance of a happy life—good health and a bad memory.'

On the state of modern journalism and her own choices of reading material: 'Journalism is worse than it used to be because it is increasingly middle class, therefore bland. I prefer individual tabloids, the *News of the World*, and individual broadsheets, *The Guardian*. I can't say that I prefer either category.'

Journalists she rates: 'I love Zoe Williams, Cathy Bennett, Jane Moore, Suzanne Moore, Jim Shelley, Geoffrey Wheatcroft—loads of people.'

Working for the *News of the World*: 'I work for the NOTW because of a) the money and b) Rebekah Wade (now editor of the *Sun*).'

From her large thirties home in Hove, complete with picture of Josef Stalin with the Spice Girls on the mantelpiece, Julie abides by the London dockers' motto 'work to live, don't live to work'. She calls Blair's revolution 'socialism for the rich and capitalism for the poor'.

Talking about *Man and Boy*, she says: 'I'm pleased that at 49, on his fifth attempt, he's finally got a best-seller 'cos I had one at 29 and jealousy's not good for a person. Eats you up!'

She once said you could never be too thin and anti-American but now she is fat and proud and holidays in Florida. A mass of contradictions. On her youth she said: 'When I was younger I was the sweetest chick in town and had a 38 inch chest and a narrow waist and what did it get me?—Tony Parsons! Now I'm ageing, I've got a 27-year-old boyfriend (Dan Raven, the brother of Julie's former 'lesbian lover' Charlotte Raven) and I'm getting it five times a night.'

On leaving Tony Parsons (ironically, I met Tony approximately the day she left and probably passed her on the platform at Billericay in Essex): 'When I left Tony, I walked out of our bungalow with nothing more than a bottle of amyl nitrate, a g-string, a bust of Lenin and an attitude.'

On journalists: 'I like hacks and am proud to call myself one—but the reason I like us is that we're one of the last pockets of louche, loose living left in an increasingly regimented world. We stay out late, sleep in even later, drink and smoke and cop off with each other at the drop of an H. Most of us became hacks not because of any great calling, but because we found it hard to get up in the morning.'

But it is her fear and loathing of the insufferable Blair which brings out her worst venom in her *Guardian* columns. 'Blair has often been accused of being almost girlishly impressed by extreme wealth, and the other side of this is what appears to be a very real dislike of the low-paid, as though being poor is somehow "dirty" or infectious. You never get the feeling that he loathes parasitical, state-welching fat cats in the way he loathes men whose only sin is to be overly willing to rush into burning buildings and rescue complete strangers.'

Irascible, provocative, hilariously outrageous and controversial, she manages to inject fresh insights into every subject she turns to: America, 'one big Manson family ... the world's dustbin'; the housewife, 'a treacherous parody of the human female'; and the Tories, 'the natural party of the under-educated and their brash anti-idealistic, anti-cerebral world view'. With Julie Burchill, it's a case of love it or shove it.

7: Red-tops and readers

ONE editor with as high a profile as Rebekah Wade is the man on the Damascan road to recovery—Piers Morgan. As esteemed media commentator Peter Preston said *in The Observer,* 'Well, transformations sometimes happen. The original *Daily Mirror,* remember, was Alfred Harmsworth's "ladies' journal" for typists and secretaries: the sixties *Mail* was flat on its broadsheet back before David English gave it a tabloid kiss of life. Polishing up the *Mirror's* image now, under 'cover of flannel, will be difficult but not impossible.'

Preston went on to maintain there's a sense to such transition. Our 'red top' tabloids are shrinking badly. The *Sun's* circulation fell to 3.5m in January 2002. Not long ago it sold more than 4m. The *Mirror* managed 2.16m that month. It's a long time since the glory days of 5.2m.

If you're Trinity's troubled management watching national ads fade away by 13 per cent, you need a meaty bone for the analysts to chew over. Editor Piers Morgan's conversion to 'real' journalism or taking the *Mirror* back to its roots after September 11 hasn't faded as fast as the cynics predicted. His *Mirror* was 4.3 per cent up month on month in January 2002 and, more tellingly, it was up 0.71 per cent year on year. As the late, great Ian Dury said, 'Hope springs eternal—right up your behind.'

Worryingly, looking at Middle England's choice, the *Daily Mail,* in the latest National Readership Survey, its circulation is rising. It has 5.69m readers, 65 per cent of them in the ad-cherished ABC1 group—more than *The Times, Independent, Guardian* and the FT rolled into one. It has three times more readers under the age of 34 than the *Daily Telegraph,* and 15 times more than *The Independent.* It is, moreover, the only national that seems to have solved the problem of female readers: an envied 52 per cent of *Mail* readers are women.

That is the opposite of the *Mirror* profile. It has 5.706m readers, but 54.2 per cent of them are men, and that shift is growing. Still more alarmingly for the ad men, 27.6 per cent of its readers are C2s, 24.6 per cent Ds and 11 per cent Es—63.2 per cent in all. The *Mirror* remains the paper of the working man. Not the typical ad agency dream.

But the *Mirror* and *Mail* share one link that must trouble both Morgan and *Mail* editor Paul Dacre. Their readers are ageing too fast. Despite the figures above, 23 per cent of *Mail* readers—1.325m—are over 65; 40 per cent are over 55. Only 24 per cent are under 34, as opposed to 37 per cent of *Guardian* readers and 31 per cent of *Times* readers. The *Mail* doesn't have an age problem to equal the dire straits of the *Telegraph:* but it does have a problem.

And so does the *Mirror.* Almost 23 per cent of its readers are over 65, just like the *Mail,* and 37 per cent are over 55. The youth end is a bit better (31 per cent under 34), which may explain why Morgan finds his readers a touch more serious-minded than Rebekah Wade's low-brow *Sun* millions.

Thus the difficulties spread. Older readers aren't as fickle in their buying or switching habits. Papers 'for men' don't turn into papers 'for women' overnight (or, looking at David English's Houdini-style *Mail* rescue act, over less than a decade). The *Mirror* and *Mail* audiences aren't a social or aspirational match. Nor, turning through page by page analysis, are the rival editorial content.

The *Mail* cares about reader research. It caters *ad nauseam* for (late) mums at home and middle-aged, middle-class, middle-brow women anxious about their shape and health. Weed out the political lead stories from a sample few weeks and here's what remains—the alarmist: 'Diabetes threat to couch potato children', 'Bottom of the heart bypass league'; or the insulting: 'My baby was killed by NHS Direct' (a service which has almost certainly saved the life of both my children). The obsession with 'pear-shaped' hips is instinctive and instructive. And when Anita Roddick puts the *Daily Mail* (or *Daily Hell* as Burchill calls it) into Room 101 as the most bigoted paper in the country, something's not right.

Sales of broadsheet newspapers have crashed to record lows, according to figures out recently. Sales of the *Daily Mirror* smashed all records in 2003 with the Paul Burrell revelations, but the so-called 'serious' papers have bombed dramatically. Ironically, although they all carry weekly expert media columns, not one of them has told the story of their circulation crisis. *The Guardian* plunged by 8.4 per cent in a year, *The Independent* by 9.4 per cent, the *Telegraph* by 5.4 per cent, *The Financial Times* by 5.3 per cent and *The Times*, in the six-month analysis period, by 2.6 per cent.

On Sundays, the situation is just as bad with the *Independent on Sunday* collapsing by 14 per cent, the *Sunday Times* by 3.2 per cent, the *Sunday Telegraph* by 4.8 per cent, and *The Observer,* taking the six-month period, by 1.6 per cent. The *Daily Mail* had also declined by 3 per cent on the previous year, and the *Mail on Sunday* by 3.7 per cent. As for the *Daily Express* and *Sunday Express,* and the *Daily Star* ... well, who cares really?

In 2002 Piers Morgan won 'newspaper of the year' awards for the more serious, campaigning nature of the paper and re-recruiting the finest investigative reporters John Pilger and Paul Foot to question the wisdom of the last 'war on terrorism'. I have never seen the *Mirror* look in better shape.

At the start of the countdown to war with Iraq, John Pilger once again got the front page splash with the headline 'Hypocrite – how dare George Bush preach peace to Israel when he's meeting Blair to plan war on Iraq ... and the deaths of thousands more innocent people' with the wonderful Pilger line 'in this country there is an honourable rallying call—not in our name'. Truly radical stuff—which only the *Mirror* is doing. Can you imagine any other tabloid in the country daring to write a story like that?

Meanwhile, it has re-branded itself back to being the *Daily Mirror* and distanced itself from the bottom-of-the-range red-tops (such as the *Sun* and *Star*) to be a campaigning paper for the mid-market. New freelance writers who mostly work for *The Guardian* such as Jim Shelley (the best TV critic in the country bar none), Jonathan Freedland, Christopher Hitchens (*Vanity Fair*) and Matthew Norman (*Guardian* diarist and *Evening Standard* columnist) have joined the ranks of Parsons, Reade, Jonathan Ross, Victor Lewis Smith, Miranda Sawyer and Bill Borrows. A new Cassandra, the legendary *Mirror* columnist, has returned to provide an insight into everyday life. Even the *Sun* is following suit by being slightly more inclusive and tolerant than in the MacKenzie era.

Leading media authority Roy Greenslade in an article in *The Guardian* showed that newspaper circulation figures fell in 2002, continuing a historic downward trend. The annual figures show a decline in both the daily and Sunday market. That doesn't mean a disaster, with more than 13m national titles still being sold every day, and taking into account the fact that the previous year's figures included the huge September 11 sales surge. But the UK print media are still declining and it's important to ask why.

Who's to blame? The government, the owners, the journalists, the buying public? Probably all of those. Only the *Daily Star* with its diet of soap stars, footballers and Kylie's arse on every cover has slightly bucked the trend in the circulation wars. They would say the *Mirror* relaunch into a serious paper has made it vulnerable. Piers Morgan quite rightly will take exception to that. Ironically, his most successful circulation issue was the less-than-serious Paul Burrell exclusive.

Whether a huge success or not, what makes the *Mirror* re-branding so interesting is the notion that papers cannot stay still any longer; they have to look for change and as the *Mirror* advertising strapline would have it 'Think Again'.

The national newspaper industry is in decline, but it's not irreversible. Owners and editors face all sorts of challenges. Distribution, for example is a problem because more papers are being sold at supermarkets and petrol stations while small corner-shop newsagents are closing. That threatens deliveries from the paper boy/girl to your home, the essence of regular sales.

Then there is the rise of a free-sheet culture. Free papers, or papers sold for almost nothing, create in the public mind a feeling of something for nothing. Yet paid-for papers go on expanding in size, offering more sections and supplements than anyone can possibly read in a day. So the economics of producing papers goes up while the price people want to pay goes down. Some cerebrally challenged people also feel that their TV news and entertainment is 'free', so ask 'why buy a paper?', forgetting the tangible reward of a newspaper.

The other major threat is the internet. Increasing numbers of people log on every day, surfing through their favourite sites. Titles that have already started online newspapers will also be in a good position to make the switch from newsprint to chargeable news internet which many predict will be a reality. But the danger of this would be a 'have and have not' information culture.

Many predicted that the major revolution in the British press would be the gradual disappearance of red-top tabloids and the upsurge of quality broadsheets. But there is still a big readership for red-tops, and broadsheets haven't capitalised on their decline.

In 2003 newspapers will have to think more about the direction in which they're heading. In that sense, however snobbish some commentators might be about Morgan's *Mirror* or staggered at *The Guardian's* rate of investment in its websites, these papers are trying to find a niche. If the *Mirror* becomes the thinking person's middle-brow *Daily Mail*, so be it.

If you wonder why modern newspapers appear to be in a state of constant change, look at the declining figures of their circulation in 2003. To try to reverse this downward trend some owners and editors have decided to spout the business cliché: innovate or die. It's not a guarantee of success, of course, because innovative thinking could just as easily cause a slow death.

A couple of editors had reasons to be cheerful—Morgan and the *Express's* Chris Williams—because they achieved monthly rises in August 2003, though still couldn't match the previous year's figure. Evidently, both gained from their controversial buy-ups, Morgan with Tony Martin, the farmer who killed a burglar, and Williams with the disgraced TV presenter, John Leslie. One bit of good news in 2003: so bad is the current situation that the scare-mongering *Daily Mail,* whose circulation was on the ascendancy, has now stopped growing.

Worryingly, the big success story in 2003 is the *Daily Star* (who I promised I wouldn't talk about but am) which is climbing towards a million sales. Producing a paper with virtually no serious content, it is a sad comment on our dumb and dumber society that the *Star* is shining. One bad trend is that its owner, Richard Desmond, has tried to show that it is possible to publish a daily paper with very few journalists.

That greed-is-good philosophy has taken root at Trinity-Mirror where the new chief executive, Sly Bailey, has instituted a cost-cutting regime which led to the announcement of 48 editorial redundancies at the *Daily Mirror,* only sixteen of which would be voluntary. These cuts would inevitably make it much harder for the *Mirror* to produce challenging, radical work. The jury is out on the *Mirror.*

Mass sackings—a regular event at the *Daily Express* over the past 25 years—indicate a dismal failure. It may please shareholders but lowers the morale of the staff, and editors know they cannot produce a serious paper with staff shortages. The cheap and nasty *Daily Star* route seems to be the way the tabloids are going now.

But the *Mirror* is back to its roots and amen to that. It is the only tabloid worth reading when you consider the red-tops. The *Star* thinks the most important news item is 'free chips for every reader', the *Sun* is slowly dragging itself into the 21st century, and the *Mail* and to a lesser extent the *Express* continue with traditional xenophobia, homophobia and any other phobia you care to mention. (The *Mail* cleverly uses conservative black faces to write racist filth, and conservative gays to peddle gay-bashing nonsense.) On the broadsheet side, the *Telegraph* remains essential reading for retired colonels, with old editor Charles Moore's Old Etonian agenda to the fore (and with Martin Newland at the helm); *The Times* has lost its campaigning teeth (from the old 'Insight' days); and only *The Guardian, Observer* and *Independent* from the broadsheets represent splendid, and meticulous newspaper coverage: in an ideal world, these would be the papers that everyone reads.

I came into journalism wide-eyed and hopeful, and came out wild-eyed and hopeless. I had my fill of the mad adrenalin-fuelled fever of working for newspapers. It wasn't all the celluloid dream of classics such as *Ace in the Hole* and *All the President's Men* with tight deadlines, camaraderie, turning inky copy round quickly, seeing your byline in print and the hate mail flooding in. Allow me a little diversion about the misconceptions on stage and screen.

As *The Guardian*'s Alfred Hickling has said, journalists have had a bad press in showbiz since 1928. Just look at the opening scene of

Howard Brenton and David Hare's 1985 Fleet Street satire, *Pravda,* for evidence.

Rebecca: When you say work ... to be honest my heart is slightly sinking.

Andrew: Yes. I'm a journalist.

Rebecca: Fuck.

Hollywood has always given journalists the short straw. Journalists are either cynical, manipulative, overweight and, very, very drunk or in dirty macs with bitten fingernails who always wear pork-pie hats indoors with a press ticket inserted. There are honourable exceptions such as *Salvador, Reds, The China Syndrome* and *The Insider* but reporters usually in the movies/soaps are incapable of being teetotal or compassionate, and easily top the list of most hated professions, even though—as Ruth, a character in Tom Stoppard's comedy *Night and Day*—admits, most people have never met a reporter in real life. 'I've always wanted to meet a journalist,' Ruth says. 'I mean socially, I don't mean under one's bed or outside the law courts. One is not normally introduced to journalists.'

The lazy stereotype of the shit-faced reporter emerged not in Hollywood, but on Broadway: in Ben Hecht and Charles MacArthur's 1928 smash, *The Front Page*, detailing the authors' experiences as hot-shot hacks in the Chicago era of speakeasys, prohibition and Al Capone. Hecht and MacArthur set the mould for all portrayals of newspapermen on stage and screen.

The image was of 'a load of lousy, daffy buttinskis swelling around with holes in their pants, all so a million hired girls and motormen's wives will know what's going on'. This was a common theme throughout the 'golden era' of newspaper films, 1928-35. The reporter had a sex change in 1939 for Howard Hawks's *His Girl Friday.* Once again the movies reinforced the stereotype about reporters being callous hard-nosed monsters: 'They're newspaper men,' Hildy explains. 'They can't help themselves. The Lord made them that way.'

The glamour and mystique of reporting that attracted me to the profession often led to disappointment. In Brenton and Hare's *Pravda,* the ambitious reporter talks about his love of 'the smell of hot type, the thunder of the foundry, the nightly rush for the first edition'. And yet the reality of reporting more often turns out to be a dreary round of council meetings and WI reports.

David Nobbs in *Pratt of the Argus* sums it up: 'There are some people who are journalists because they possess an enquiring mind and are burning with a driving need to comment on the world around them. There are others who are journalists because they are idiots.'

Stoppard, who began his career as a cub reporter on a local paper, recalls that his first ambition was to be 'lying on the floor of an African airport while machine-gun bullets zoomed over my typewriter'. Also from Stoppard's *Night and Day*: 'If you've got a free press, everything is correctable, and without it everything is concealable.' To which his hostess Ruth makes an apposite reply: 'I'm with you on the free press. It's the newspapers I can't stand.'

8: The sultans of spin

I WAS lucky to have been part of the most exciting period in British journalism. Now we see the ever-increasing tabloidisation and dumbing down of the print media. The once-great NME and *Mirror* now get a much smaller audience than I used to write for (in its heyday the NME captured a million people weekly and the *Daily Mirror* ten million daily). I can remember a time when newspapers used to carry real stories—not celebrity trivia such as 'footballer in cocaine scandal' and 'rock star and prostitute shock'—which are complete non-stories to my mind. As MP Austin Mitchell says in his book *The Case for Labour*, papers fawn on power rather than questioning it, and trivialise without seeking to explain or understand. He concludes the right-wing bias comes from a combination of sycophancy and ownership structure. As he says, 'They pander to our ignorance and feed our prejudices back to us amplified and made respectable.'

Whether it be anti-immigrant, anti-scrounger, anti-union, it is always salacious and jingoistic. The inane nationalism of 'Kill an Argy, win a Metro' *Sun* mood of the Falklands crisis or the ludicrous *Daily Mail* headline 'Liberators' after the Iraq crisis (when clearly the local Iraqi people regarded the Americans as an occupying force) would make outsiders think we were not a tolerant, fair-minded people (which we undoubtedly are) but a xenophobic war-like nation. The *Daily Star* probably covered the entire waterfront of dumbed-down journalism with its headline 'Asylum seekers ate my donkey'.

After these excesses it was difficult to believe anything you read in the tabloids. It conjured up the old stand-up gag about what's the difference between the *Sun* and the *Beano*—5 pence! I remember hearing Jack Jones talking about one of the well-attended marches to restore the earnings link to pensions and commenting on the lack of media coverage, saying 'the only way they'll put this on the BBC news is if we put a brick through McDonalds'. Needless to say, he didn't and nothing was shown on the broadcast media at all. Nor is there much trust attached to journalists. Ian Mayes from *The Guardian* wrote an excellent piece on this very subject.

He asked: how far would you trust a journalist? He mentioned a Steve Bell cartoon, drawn in the style of the fabulous seaside postcards of Donald McGill. The cartoon shows two men leaning over the promenade rail. One is in a pinstriped suit. The other is in a shabby mac with a 'press' ticket stuck in the band of his trilby. He is saying: 'Remind me, minister, am I the sewer or the sewage?'

Journalists are prone to describing themselves as 'hacks' and 'scribblers' only partly in self-loathing. The public they serve generally view them, thanks to ludicrous TV and film depictions, as the lowest of the low, the slime of the slime. This is nothing new. Dr Johnson once said: 'In Sir Henry Wotton's jocular definition, "an ambassador" is said to be "a man of virtue sent abroad to tell lies for the advantage of his country"; a news-writer is a man without virtue who writes lies at home for his own profit.'

Dr Johnson rubs further salt in the wound: 'To these compositions is required neither genius nor knowledge, neither industry nor sprightliness, but contempt of shame, and indifference to truth are absolutely necessary. He who ... has obtained these qualities may confidently tell today what he intends to contradict tomorrow.'

Two hundred years later, journalists still do not stand high in public opinion. Mori, which has been gauging levels of trust in various professions and other groups since 1983, has produced consistently disheartening results. In answer to the question, 'Tell me whether you generally trust [journalists] to tell the truth or not?' the majority have said no.

The old joke runs: 'How do you stop a journalist from drowning? ... Take your foot off his head!' Journalists invariably come out very close to the bottom of the Mori poll, usually a little below estate agents, lawyers and politicians. Only one in five people said they did trust journalists but none of the polls cited distinguishes between journalists by medium or by type of publication. In spring of 2003, however, a poll which did make these distinctions, conducted by YouGov for the *Daily Telegraph,* published different results.

The question again was: 'How much do you trust the following to tell the truth ... ?' Broadcast journalists in ITV News, BBC News and Channel 4 News came out among the most trusted groups, with 81 per cent saying they trusted them a great deal or a fair amount and only 17 per cent saying not much or not at all—giving a net trust figure of 64 per cent.

For journalists on broadsheet papers such as the *Daily Telegraph, The Times* and *The Guardian,* the figures were 65 per cent trusting them a great deal or a fair amount; 34 per cent not very much or not at all; net trust 31 per cent. Journalists on local newspapers came only a little lower. The net trust figure for journalists on mid-market papers such as the *Mail* and *Express* was minus-26; and, right at the bottom of the poll, for journalists on the 'red-top' tabloids, the net trust figure was minus-69.

Anthony King, professor of government at Essex University, analysing the results of the poll in the *Daily Telegraph,* declared that with them 'one of the great myths of British public life is blown sky-high'—namely that **all** journalists are held in the same low esteem, as low as estate agents and politicians. Professor King said that broadcast journalists were among the most trusted of professionals and that reporters on broadsheet newspapers ranked just below judges.

Back to Mori and to Ian Mayes from *The Guardian*. 'All its polls since 1983 show that people are far more inclined to trust "the ordinary man or woman in the street" to tell them the truth than the generality of journalists. Journalists, however—if it is a conclusion that can be drawn from the YouGov poll—seem to rise in public trust as the "public service" element in their work increases.' Alan Rusbridger, editor of *The Guardian*, added that newspapers which sermonised needed to face up to their own failings.

'Sack the hack,' demands the Sun, calling the BBC's Andrew Gilligan 'a second-rate journalist who cannot be trusted'. Which is a case of pots and kettles, as shown by the most recent research on who the public most trusts to tell the truth. Ironically, the BBC is far superior to the *Sun* in terms of believability, according to the public. BBC1 scores 92 per cent, the *Sun* 11 per cent. The truth about most journalism is that it is (in the memorable words of the *Washington Post*'s David Broder) 'partial, hasty, incomplete, inevitably somewhat flawed and inaccurate'.

Polls on the Iraq war coverage are even more interesting. Roy Greenslade in *The Guardian* recently reviewed the evidence of a new poll which showed that although the *Mirror* is opposed to the war, and unlike any time in its history has not backed the war when the bombing began, half its readers are in favour. The polling company ICM asked people whether they approved/disapproved of the war and then found out which daily newspapers each respondent regularly reads.

What Greenslade found most striking was the fact that there were significant minorities opposed to the war among the readers of the most gung-ho, war-mongering papers and *vice versa*. For instance, a quarter of the *Daily Mail*'s readership disapproved of the war, and a quarter of *The Guardian*'s approved of it.

The journalists on the *Daily Telegraph*, which was resolutely supportive of the war, may be staggered to learn that more than a third of its readers do not agree with its editorial line. The *Telegraph* published a letter from a former Bomber Command pilot, which was one of the most passionate anti-war statements I have seen, arguing that he was ashamed by Britain's 'illegal and hypocritical aggression against Iraq'. It is evident from the poll that the anti-war *Independent* also had more than a third of pro-war readers.

The Independent's circulation (before its tabloid downsizing) increased during the war, claiming about 9 per cent extra on its daily sale in one week. *The Guardian* reported a rise in sales since hostilities began, as did *The Times*. The *Daily Telegraph* did not fare as well. The tabloids have not found as much interest among their target audiences.

The *Daily Mirror*, which reports a 'reasonable' sales increase, is the paper that has returned the most surprising ICM poll result of any title. It ran a sensational and high-profile campaign against the war. But 49% of its readers evidently supported the war, while only 38% disapproved of it. Piers Morgan does, rightly, point out that the poll was conducted after the war had started, and there had been a noticeable shift of support in Tony Blair's favour since then.

To an extent, Morgan's *Mirror* reflected that by switching from the Blair 'Blood on his hands' pre-war splash and concentrating its attack instead on Bush, over a front-page picture of a grinning president and, beneath, a weeping Iraqi bomb victim, headlined 'He loves it'. Despite the poll, Morgan said his mailbag was running 80/20 in favour of the *Mirror*'s line, and the daily selection of published letters demonstrates that.

There is no sign of uncertainty among the *Sun*'s white-van man readership. Its 68 per cent approval rating for the war was the highest among any paper and its 17 per cent disapproval rating the lowest. But what would the results have shown, a month before the war, when public opinion in the huge two million-strong march and the polls, demonstrated a majority against war. The first casualty of war is the truth and that might be the same for this poll, which is ambiguous to say the least.

Piers Morgan told Peter Preston in *The Observer*. 'I personally slightly misjudged the way you could be attitudinal on the front page once the war started,' he said. 'We caught a bit of a cold to be honest.' With his circulation declining and future in doubt, this was a sad reflection on the boldest *Mirror* to have hit the news-stands for ages.

Morgan added about the circulation decline: 'I would say that the rate of decline is significantly less than it used to be—and that we've done, in my view, a bloody good job in keeping it where it's been.

'My early strategy of trying to out-*Sun* the *Sun* was not a brilliant success. In fact, it was virtually a total disaster, culminating in "Achtung! Surrender" and enough opprobrium to wilt a forest of oak trees.

'Mirror readers didn't really hanker for the buckets of trashy, racy, celeb-driven scandal sleaze I was serving up. They wanted more substance. They wanted hard news, authoritative comment, strong features—and above all a loud, coherent, campaigning, radical and attitudinal voice.

'It wasn't that they were boring or that they were uninterested in celebrities. They just wanted their *Mirror* to put those things into perspective and not bill them constantly as the most important thing of the day.'

Is the *Mirror* a more 'serious' paper, or not? If it is, it needs to look slightly more serious—fresh typefaces, fresh feel and it needs to edge into middle-market territory, away from a *Sun,* which can outgun it in price wars and tabloid 'screamers'.

Can Morgan, given time and support, begin to work that transformation? Possibly. Nobody else has his impeccable Fleet Street credentials. The real challenge is public perception of newspaper value. Sly Bailey, chief executive at Trinity Mirror which owns the *Mirror* group, has pleased City analysts and shareholders with her hardball talk of cost-cutting and 'innovation' at the *Mirror.* But strip away the corporate gobbledegook and does it all mean massive job losses and a return to low-rent journalism where a celebrity fest will replace challenging, radical reporting? Only time will tell. Early signs are that circulation is rising again. The *Mirror,* despite its opposition to his seemingly crazed vigilantism, bought the biggest populist story of the year with the release of Norfolk farmer Tony Martin, freed after four years in jail, after shooting dead a 16-year-old burglar.

His story, which was pure tabloidese, started a national debate over whether anyone has any right to kill someone to defend their property. It pushed the *Mirror's* sales to just over 2m copies per day. But this wasn't breaking the biggest stories—it was just providing the biggest cheque-book, although Martin claimed he could have got more money elsewhere and the *Mirror* was a paper he could trust. Or was that more spin?

CP Scott, the legendary *Guardian* editor, wrote in 1921:

> The primary office of a newspaper is the gathering of news. At the peril of its soul it must see that the supply is not tainted. Neither in what it gives, nor in what it does not give, nor in the mode of presentation, must the unclouded face of truth suffer wrong.

And as Patrick Weever in *The Observer* argued in the middle of the awesome duel between the government and the BBC over the 'sexed-up' Iraq dossier, Scott's values are worth considering. The next sentences in that famous essay, to celebrate the 100th anniversary of *The Guardian,* ring true today:

> Comment is free, but facts are sacred ... The voice of opponents no less than that of friends has a right to be heard ... It is well to be frank, it is even better to be fair.

The growing numbers of the great anti-spin movement in this country may moan that we have travelled a great way since Scott's time—and nearly always in the wrong direction. Weever, a former business editor of the *Independent on Sunday,* launched a website called *Anti-Spin.com.* Its aim is to provide a space for those writers who believe that our world is being swamped by propaganda, deception and half-truths, to see whether this is really happening, and, if so, find out why.

But what is spin? In America it's applauded—in the UK it is derided. *Financial Times* writer John Lloyd says that to the journalist, spin is 'spinning away from the truth'. But, says Lloyd, the government minister, politician or indeed businessman or celebrity has a diametrically opposed view. To him, or her, spin is a necessary guard against the excesses of a terrifying and sometimes destructive free press. At its worst it can lead to tragedies such as the death of the government mole, Dr David Kelly.

* * * *

What we are witnessing in many ways is what is called the PR-isation of the media. The independence of journalists can be called into question as they become more dependent on partisan sources, without this being made clear to their readers. This dependence means that their ability to question and analyse is being challenged by public relations practitioners who wield real power.

Furthermore, the media industry itself is complicit. The proportion of news coverage is declining with more and more space being devolved to the puerile, voyeuristic and trivial—the dumbing down of the media.

Lazy journalists are happy to accept pre-written copy without challenge and take the easy option by not checking the facts for themselves or by not finding opposing voices.

Surprisingly, these are the words of Professor Anne Gregory, the president-elect of the Institute of Public Relations. But these views would probably be shared by the personable, Groucho Marx lookalike, David Hill, the current Blair communications director who interviewed me for a job in the Labour Party in 1997 and who switched, ironically, to work for Thatcher's favourite PR man Sir Tim Bell. They are also echoed by former Labour spin-meister Charlie Whelan who I also met and who says in *PR Week*: 'Alastair Campbell knows the media love nothing better than a story about itself and is particularly obsessed with spin-doctors ... Campbell wanted headlines to deflect attention away from his boss. A weapon of mass distraction.'

The investigative journalist, Phillip Knightley, under Harry Evans' editorship at the *Sunday Times,* has a different take on it. 'One day, the owner of the paper, a Canadian called Lord Thompson, knocked on the editor's door while the morning news conference was in progress, said "hello", and then rather tentatively asked: "Say boys, would it be possible to squeeze in the Canadian ice hockey results each Sunday?"

'There was a moment of shocked silence. Then the deputy editor, Hugo Young, said, "Lord Thompson, this is an editorial news conference to which you've not been invited. If you'd like to put your suggestion in writing, I'm sure that the sports editor will be willing to consider it." And next morning there was a note to the editor from Thompson apologising for attempting to interfere with the paper's editorial policy.

'Can you imagine Rupert Murdoch ever doing such a thing?'
Exactly.

The *Hindu Times* (no, not the Oasis single) ran a leader by Hasan Suroor where it said that 'the Culture of 'spin' is at the heart of the perpetual Blair-media tension ... Nothing that comes out of Downing Street is taken at face value any more.'

It went on to say that the one area which governments found particularly hard to handle was their relationship with the media. Even more so, when the press is combative and starts to fancy itself as a substitute for a weak Opposition. Faced with relentless media assaults not on just policy issues but on individuals and their private lives, the governments begin to suspect the media's motives.

Tony Blair fights almost daily battles with an aggressive and intrusive media but still controls the Tory press (because, as Bob Crow, the RMT union leader, replied when asked 'Aren't you worried about letting the Tories in?', 'who'd notice the difference?'). But there are limits beyond which a government with a popular mandate to govern cannot allow itself to be 'bullied' by journalists who, for all their admirable zeal to clean up society, in the end represent no-one but private—and in many cases politically motivated—interests. I'm thinking of Murdoch's anti-euro agenda.

The argument has not been easy to win, however, as the government discovered to its exasperation and embarrassment. In a test case, Downing Street reported three Tory publications to the Press Complaints Commission over allegations that Mr Blair's office put pressure on a Palace official to get a more prominent role for him at the Queen Mother's funeral. But, within weeks, it had to drop the case. The fact is that its first major attempt to 'discipline' the press failed miserably. Maybe, it picked on the wrong issue, but as one Labour supporter said, 'It proves that you should never ever take on the press.'

But let's go back to where the roots of the Blair-media confrontation lie—in Downing Street and Alastair Campbell, whose job, to put it crudely, was to 'manipulate' news in favour of his boss and the government. As they say in PR circles 'perception is reality'. I used to see the ebullient Campbell ranting and raving at the *Mirror* office and I admired the way he helped get Labour elected in 1997—writing to him and mentioning I knew him from *Mirror* days. Surprisingly, he replied and said 'thanks for your very kind words' in a quite considerate note (very unlike the caricature of Campbell as the king of spin and a bully). But he was always slightly more left-wing than Blair, and his successor David Hill, even though he is not a socialist, is a man I know and respect. But even then 'these pretty straight guys' (as Nick Cohen ironically describes them) seem to have a passion to manipulate the truth.

Campbell was nicknamed the '*de facto* Deputy Prime Minister'. But it was his aggressive approach to news management which made him notoriously famous, gave a dubious new interpretation to the word 'spin', alienated journalists and did as much to damage the government's image as its increasingly unpopular policies or actions.

The government blames this on a 'cynical' press which, according to cabinet minister Charles Clarke, is set to bring 'democratic politics into disrepute' by constantly talking about 'sleaze' and 'spin'. Critics, on the other hand, accuse New Labour of 'paranoia' and 'intolerance' despite the Blair government's strong position, especially after a second landslide election victory.

Spin-on-this.com spoofed Blair and his relationship with the media brilliantly. 'Tony Blair says he has no memory of tanks being deployed at Heathrow airport in an effort to scare the British public shitless. Mr Blair has also denied he ever mentioned that Saddam Hussein was about to nuke the crap out of the "Western World" with his special "anthrax ricin bouncing bomb machine". In fact, Mr Blair says he's not sure whether the whole idea of a war in Iraq isn't just "something got up by the BBC". Blair—sporting a rictus grin—insisted, "I believe sincerely that every time I say 'I believe sincerely' the British media will always believe me sincerely. This is because thanks to extensive propaganda and church attendance, I'm apparently the only politician in the world who isn't a power-crazed corrupt lying bastard."'

With the suicide of David Kelly, who the *Mirror* claimed was 'spun to death', and the departure of Campbell, the sultans of spin went into overdrive. In a statement Campbell said his family had paid a high price for his high-profile role in Downing Street, but that it had been an 'enormous privilege to work so closely in opposition and in government for someone I believe history will judge as a great transforming prime minister'. While Campbell's resignation came as a shock, before the Hutton inquiry there was a widespread view that he had become a liability to Blair. Probably not: Campbell was an expert in news management but an integral part of that tainted brand—the New Labour Project. His was certainly a very high-pressure job, but when half the people tell the pollsters that they don't believe a single word the Prime Minister says, the buck has to stop either with the PM or with Alastair Campbell, doesn't it?

Welsh Assembly Leader Rhodri Morgan said before Campbell's departure: 'I think what is important is that he is a key member of the Praetorian Guard, equal to Peter Mandelson. Mandelson's out of the cabinet, Milburn and Byers are out of the cabinet, Anji Hunter has gone. If Alastair Campbell goes, really only Jonathan Powell perhaps of the original Praetorian Guard will still be there whenever Alastair actually finally does cut his links.

'...it leaves Tony Blair really with two years to build up a new Praetorian Guard. But each member of the Praetorian Guard is different. I've never been convinced that Alastair Campbell is New Labour. He's certainly intensely loyal, we saw that, even to people like Robert Maxwell; he's intensely loyal to Tony Blair and will never do anything to harm Tony Blair.'

But it's a pity Campbell didn't listen to the advice he gave Gordon Brown's former spin doctor, Charlie Whelan. He said when the spin-doctor becomes the story, then it's time for him to go. Paul Routledge, the *Mirror's* Chief Political Commentator and the best champion for real Labour in the tabloids, added about Campbell's departure: 'Finally, he did the right thing. If only we could believe that he did it for the right reasons.'

The timing of his resignation was perfect. It came only hours after Tony Blair's awkward appearance before the Hutton inquiry, and brilliantly span attention away from the political trials and tribulations of the Prime Minister. Just for once, it was a good thing that Campbell was the story and not his boss.

The Campbell departure has shown us many things but above all that the relationship between government and media is so crucial to the future of democracy. There is much to explain, especially the way in which newspapers spun so successfully against what they deemed to be the concept of spin. There is also the problem of a media industry which has labelled all politicians as charlatans and encouraged an apathetic electorate. The crisis of representation continues

The fallout from the Hutton report did serious damage to the journalistic profession. As Martin Kettle writing in *The Guardian* said about the whole Hutton saga: 'Having read the Hutton report and most of what has been written about it, I have reached the following, strictly non-judicial, conclusions: first, that the episode illuminates a wider crisis in British journalism than the turmoil at the BBC; second, that too many journalists are in denial about this wider crisis; third, that journalists need to be at the forefront of trying to rectify it; and, fourth, that this will almost certainly not happen.'

He goes on to say that, the more you read it, the more you get the sense that the modern journalist is prone to behaving like a child throwing its toys out of the pram when it doesn't get what it wants. He talks about journalistic scorn and prejudice. There was rattle-throwing from the right of the cot—'a great disservice to the British nation' (Sir Max Hastings in the *Daily Mail)*—and from the left—'Lord Whitewash' (Paul Routledge in the *Daily Mirror*). Rod Liddle writing in *The Spectator* went further: 'I think, as a country, we've had enough of law lords.' *The Economist* had a different take on Gilligan: 'Typical of much of modern British journalism, twisting or falsifying the supposed news to fit a journalist's opinion about where the truth really lies. Some in the British media have described such journalism as "brave". Sloppy or biased would be better words.' While *Financial Times* editor Andrew Gowers, described this 'dreadful misadventure' as a wake-up call for British journalism, and said it 'should prompt us to resist the easy, superficial certainties of partisan opinion and rediscover the virtues of accuracy, context and verification'.

Paul Routledge summed up my feelings when he said about Blair and Hutton: 'His judicial pal Lord Hutton has found him not guilty of all charges in the Kelly affair.' Routledge added: 'The establishment whitewash that passed for a judicial inquiry is simply not good enough. What we need is an independent inquiry by someone who is not paid by the government to investigate how and why we went to war'. Like me, he maintains that the gist of the BBC story has proved to be true. 'Even Lord Hutton, who plainly hears no evil and sees no evil, admits the spooks may have "subconsciously" hyped up the evidence to help the government's case for war,' says Routledge.

As my own union, the NUJ, and our general secretary, Jeremy Dear, said: 'The Hutton Report poses a real and grave threat to journalism. It will inevitably mean that journalists face greater pressure to reveal their sources and it will make sources and whistle-blowers think twice before coming forward.' He described as 'abject' an apology from BBC governors and said it had given succour to politicians and others who wanted to influence the news agenda. In an e-mail circulated to staff, the NUJ urged workers to 'stand up for independence and the integrity of BBC programmes'. It called for freedom from government interference, transparency in the selection of a new director-general and chairman, and demanded there should be no cuts in BBC licence fee funding.

9: Lukewarm Britannia

CABINET minister and prospective Labour leader Peter Hain urged the spinning to stop in a comment piece in the *Independent on Sunday*: 'There is a fine tradition of investigative journalism that must continue—including by broadcasters, and the BBC in particular considering its public service remit. Many genuine scandals have been exposed, and suffering and abuse ended, because of excellent journalism. There is a fine tradition of critical and campaigning journalism—and that must continue also. But when it becomes journalistic spin, it must not be dressed up as straightforward reporting—with lines blurred between fact and comment.'

He went on to say that instead of reporting, some journalists were increasingly spinning. To him intense competition means even broadsheets hugely over-hype. He said he had consistently experienced sub-editors who often wrote headlines and introductions which bore little resemblance to quoted words, which broadcasters then transmitted without correction.

He described this as a 'chicken and egg situation' where the media becomes a 24-hour rolling, non-stop machine, with producers and editors crying out for a new angle to 'take the story on'. He claimed politicians responded with media grids, pagers and pre-briefings of announcements—anything to wrest back control of the frenzied news agenda. He concludes that the endless merry-go-round sucks in everybody, including public service broadcasters.

John Pilger in the *New Statesman* talked about the state of journalism. 'There is something deeply corrupt consuming this craft of mine. It is not a recent phenomenon; look back on the 'coverage' of the First World War by journalists who were subsequently knighted for their services to the concealment of the truth of that great slaughter. What makes the difference today is the technology that produces an avalanche of repetitive information, which in the United States has been the source of arguably the most vociferous brainwashing in that country's history.'

The corruption of journalism can be seen everywhere: 'Yes, too many died in the war,' wrote leading Blair supporter Andrew Rawnsley in *The Observer*. 'Too many people always die in war. War is nasty and brutish, but at least this conflict was mercifully short. The death toll has been nothing like as high as had been widely feared. Thousands have died in the war, millions have died at the hands of Saddam.'

As Pilger argued, this is lazy journalism, where life is cheap. Saddam Hussein killed a great many people, but 'millions', like Stalin and Hitler?

David Edwards of MediaLens asked Amnesty International about this. Amnesty produced a catalogue of Saddam's killings that amounted to hundreds every year, not millions. Hussein has an appalling record that does not require the hype of state-inspired propaganda—propaganda whose aim, in Rawnsley's case, is to protect Tony Blair from the serious charges of which people all over the world believe he is guilty.

As Greg Palast once wrote, 'Blair is in the doghouse with his own Labour Party for having been caught in a fib.' The British people are a tad miffed about our leader's ludicrous fabrication of evidence that Saddam Hussein had an evil chemistry set in his basement capable of wiping out London. Even Blair's own minister calls his boss's claims about the bogus Weapons of Mass Destruction 'a bunch of Horlicks' (a very middle-class New Labour expression).

Palast noticed the Prime Minister's mad affection for all things American in his job reporting from London for BBC and *The Guardian/Observer*. As a Yank in King Tony's court, he has seen during Blair's seven years in office, what began as puppy love for Bill Clinton degenerate into pathetic poodledom at George Bush's beck and call. The Prime Minister's need to be on Bush's leash is the result of the strange politics that Blair calls 'modernisation'. Blair, you see, loathes Britain.

As Palast said, 'This Prime Minister despises his storybook countryside and its grumbling farmers with their two little pigs and their tiny fields edged with dry stone. He cringes at the little bell ringing over the door of the village post office—so quaint and so maddeningly inefficient. He cannot fathom a nation that weeps when he shuts the last filthy coal pits.'

Palast saw Blair's America fixation up close and personal in 1998 when he went undercover to investigate US corporate influence on the government for *The Observer*. Working out of an expensive hotel suite overlooking the Tower of London, he pretended to represent Blair's favourite American corporation, a notorious Texas company called ... Enron. He wanted to find out how much it would cost in 'consulting fees' to overturn England's environmental laws for the benefit of a US client.

It turned out the price for bending the rules for Enron would be ludicrously low. Palast concluded: 'Blair's ministers and cronies were selling policy changes dirt-cheap because they knew that Tony, like an amateur hooker, was giving it away for free.'

Here comes the media tie-up. From faith in Enron to faith in Enron's president is a short leap. In January 2000, just before George Bush's inauguration, Rupert Murdoch's lobbyist warned the Prime Minister that for Blair to satisfy his lust for corporate America's affection, Britain must accede as well to the new US president's military mission. The rest is history, and he will be judged on it.

Jackie Ashley in *The Guardian* argued: 'While David Kelly's family call for a pause, a bit of silence, the hysterical headlines only get wilder. There's blood on Blair's hands, or the BBC's journalism killed him, or this is the New Labour Watergate. To call for calm now is like pressing the case for a vegan diet on the wolfpack.

'The government's enemies, now led by Associated Newspapers, have accused its spin-politics of having killed Dr Kelly ... MPs on the left are particularly vitriolic, having suffered themselves from what they see as a scurrilous trait in New Labour's character—spin.'

Ashley pointed out that we have a strange alliance of interests. The attacks on the BBC have been led by two groups—Rupert Murdoch's newspapers and New Labour spin-doctors—bosom buddies for many years. The hidden Murdoch agenda is transparent: Tony, we are your real supporters, not the loony lefties of the BBC. Even after changes to the Communications Bill, Murdoch's hopes of getting a terrestrial British TV channel, and pushing out ITV, remain alive. The more the government reins in the corporation, the better for Murdoch. His papers are in cynical attack mode. Yet ironically Blair still stays in control of the media.

Except papers like the *Daily Mirror* that re-emerged following September 11 2001 into a radical, challenging newspaper and is now in danger of being taken down market by new chief executive Bailey who wants a more Blairite paper, according to my source inside the paper. Roy Greenslade, in a *Guardian* article called 'Slash and Burn', described the reinvented *Mirror* as a 'worthy', 'anti-Labour' and 'unbalanced' paper—all of which, as John Pilger explained in a response to the article, was untrue. For a year and a half, the *Mirror* gave its readers a vision of what a tabloid newspaper can be when it frees itself from the dumbing-down celebrity-driven formula that has driven away millions of newspaper readers.

Far from 'alienating' its readers, apart from a few traditional Labour right-wingers, as Greenslade claims, the *Mirror* reflected their voices on the genuine issues of concern, especially the issue of an illegal war which saw the biggest demonstration ever in this country. The *Daily Mirror* accurately represented the majority of the views of the British people, whose criticism of the Blair government's pre-war spin stole a march on the rest of the media. Instead of regurgitating New Labour press releases, the *Mirror* challenged and exposed lies—which is the role of real journalism. It was never 'anti-Labour' (just pro real Labour values) but it was anti the lies of Blair and his sidekicks. It certainly wasn't 'unbalanced': three regular columnists were pro-war (Tony Parsons, Christopher Hitchens and Sue Carroll).

As Pilger concluded in his response, 'Popular newspapers are vulnerable to price-cutting wars and it was this that saw the *Mirror*'s circulation dip, not its journalism. A not dissimilar promotional war against the *Mirror* had the same effect thirty years ago. The *Mirror* was right on the war, right on Blair and right on what a decent popular newspaper ought to be, and no amount of false received wisdom will change that.'

Max Hastings (my editor for my last month at the *Evening Standard*), writing in the *Independent on Sunday* about the Hutton inquiry, said: 'It seems unlikely to do much for the image of Tony Blair, but the first week of evidence also produced a cringe-making portrait of journalists in action.' He said that that one of the most pernicious trends in recent years had been the extension of the *Private Eye* ethic—'this story's too good to check'—to mainstream national titles and broadcasters.

Hastings continued: 'An ambitious young woman whom I was interviewing for a job once asked me if journalism was a gentleman's profession. No, no, I answered, it is a trade for cads and bounders. I was not altogether joking. Many reporters and editors would be unfit for employment in more rigorous businesses. I have been a journalist for 40 years yet I have never learnt shorthand and cannot type properly. I use a tape-recorder only for formal interviews. My notes are incomprehensible to anybody but me.' That echoes my experience, as even though I was taught Pitman's New Era shorthand, I could never read it back and decided to take a tiny tape recorder everywhere.

'Virtuous journalism is a weedy growth,' an American journalist named Michael Kirkhorn wrote wisely a few years ago in *British Journalism Review*. 'It tends to be weedily unsystematic. Virtuous journalists are much more likely to hang around ... than to practise any form of "precision journalism". Journalism is not art, it is not science—journalists practise the art of the scavenger.'

Hastings concludes: 'Yet out of the jungle of speculation, half-truth, dubious sources, shaky note-taking, inadequate fact-checking and extravagant personal ambition in which the media work, the public gets to learn many things that, if government had its way, would remain concealed. A very rough justice call must be made. On whom would you prefer to rely for your information about what our masters in Whitehall and at Westminster are doing to us: the BBC, or Alastair Campbell? I am still confident of my own answer to that one.'

As John Pilger says, 'It is not enough for journalists to see themselves as mere messengers without understanding the hidden agendas of the message and the myths that surround it.'

Corporate journalism in the United States talks about 'objectivity' and mocks those who take the side of the dispossessed and disenfranchised.

But the mainstream media in Britain make a few token allowances, with journalists like Pilger, talking to David Barsamian in *Progressive* magazine about Blair and the media, saying: 'We have an extreme right-wing government in this country, although it's called the Labour government. That's confused a lot of people, but it's confusing them less and less. The British Labour Party has always had a very strong "Atlanticist component", with an obsequiousness to American policies, and Blair represents this wing. He's clearly obsessed with Iraq. He has to be because the overwhelming majority of the people of Britain oppose a military action. I've never known a situation like it. To give you one example, The *Daily Mirror* polled its readers and 90 per cent were opposed to an attack on Iraq. Overall, opinion polls in this country are running at about 70 per cent against the war. Blair is at odds with the country.'

Talking about the *Mirror,* he added: 'I wrote for the *Mirror* for twenty years. I joined it back in the 1960s when I arrived from Australia. You don't really have anything like the *Mirror*—as it was, and as it is trying to be again—in the United States. The *Mirror* is a left-leaning tabloid. It's really a traditional supporter of the Labour Party in this country. I suppose its politics are centre-left. During the time I was there, it was very adventurous politically. It reported many parts of the world from the point of view of victims of wars. I reported Vietnam for many years for the *Mirror*. In those days, it played a central role in the political life of this country. It then fell into a long, rather terrible period, trying to copy its Murdoch rival, the *Sun*, and just became a trashy tabloid.'

Of the reinvention of the *Mirror,* he says: 'Since September 11, the *Mirror* has reached back to its roots, and decided, it seems, to be something of its old self again. I received a call asking if I would write for it again, which I've done. It's a pleasure to be able to do that. It's become an important antidote to a media that is, most of it, supportive of the establishment, some of it quite rabidly right-wing. The *Mirror* is breaking ranks, and that's good news.'

He said the *Mirror*, unlike Murdoch's *Sun,* was not read by soccer hooligans or allegedly racist killers but by ordinary people. He said he was proud to be attacked by Murdoch, who ludicrously called the *Mirror* a terrorist-supporting London paper.

On the state of journalism today, he reflects: 'Many journalists now are no more than channelers and echoers of what Orwell called the official truth. They simply cipher and transmit lies. It really grieves me that so many of my fellow journalists can be so manipulated that they become really what the French describe as *functionaires*—not journalists.

'Many journalists become very defensive when you suggest to them that they are anything but impartial and objective. The problem with those words "impartiality" and "objectivity" is that they have lost their dictionary meaning. They've been taken over. "Impartiality" and "objectivity" now mean the establishment point of view. Whenever a journalist says to me, "Oh, you don't understand, I'm impartial, I'm objective," I know what he's saying. I can decode it immediately. It means he channels the official truth. Almost always. That protestation means he speaks for a consensual view of the establishment. This is internalised. Journalists don't sit down and think, "I'm now going to speak for the establishment." Of course not. But they internalise a whole set of assumptions, and one of the most potent assumptions is that the world should be seen in terms of its usefulness to the West, not humanity.'

Pilger points out a major journalistic distinction here. 'This leads journalists to make a distinction between people who matter and people who don't matter. The people who died in the Twin Towers in that terrible crime mattered. The people who were bombed to death in dusty villages in Afghanistan didn't matter, even though it now seems that their numbers were greater. The people who will die in Iraq don't matter. Iraq has been successfully demonised as if everybody who lives there is Saddam Hussein. In the build-up to this attack on Iraq, journalists have almost universally excluded the prospect of civilian deaths, the numbers of people who would die, because those people don't matter.'

He concludes on a journalist's role: 'It's only when journalists understand the role they play in this propaganda, it's only when they realise they can't be both independent, honest journalists and agents of power, that things will begin to change.'

Matthew Norman writing in the *Mirror* thinks the game is up for Blair and his being 'economical with the truth' to the media. 'Observing Tony Blair today is like watching a man eking out his last days on Death Row. You know what's coming. All you don't know is whether the next last-minute appeal will delay it.'

Norman adds: 'He issues an advance copy of a tough Thatcheresque speech he's about to give the trade union leaders ... and then delivers a cosy, fireside chat. And this a few days after the funeral service for spin.

'It's as if Churchill had handed out copies of "we willl fight them on the beaches" to the press at 6pm, and in the Commons at 10pm declared: "We will greet them on the beaches and ask them not to be so beastly."'

Paul Foot summed up Blair perfectly when he said in *The Guardian*: 'He is exceptionally courageous when faced with his own supporters, organised trade unionists, fractious health service patients, troublesome pensioners, rowdy schoolchildren, prisoners or asylum-seekers. But as soon as he comes up against private health insurers, university chieftains, generals, intelligence spooks, industrialists, Rupert Murdoch, Bernie Ecclestone, the Hinduja brothers or the US president and his militaristic administration, Blair the Steadfast is miraculously transformed into Blair the Meek, as pliable as any Labour leader in history, including even Ramsay MacDonald. 'He is, in short, for turning. In this respect he is indeed just like Margaret Thatcher: courageous and unbending when facing up to the weak, the workers and the poor; grovelling and sycophantic to the rich, the strong and the powerful.'

'The hope that change will bring is outweighing the fear of change.' The words of one Tony Blair talking to *Vanity Fair* magazine before becoming Prime Minister. Shortly afterwards we became Cool Britannia.

As John Harris points out in *The Last Party*, his definitive book on the whole Britpop uber-cool Blair era, the phrase originated from the Bonzo Dog Doo Dah band in 1967. Zoe Williams explained in *The Guardian*: 'Labour did seem like a new dawn, Tony still had a full set of gears, and he still used verbs, even if he did put them in weird places.'

Blair, Alastair Campbell and John Prescott invited Blur's Damon Albarn to Westminster for what Arthur Daley would have called a 'Vera and philharmonic' (a G&T). It was a huge coup to get Albarn to the House of Commons in the first place. If Kinnock with his Red Wedge *débâcle* and Tracey Ullman video had asked for an audience with the trendiest Parklife creator, he would probably have been been given the shortest of shrifts. And nearly seven years later, we are no longer cool. We are a tepidly uncool Britannia.

Looking back, it is incredible how much Blair talked about popular culture in the warm-up to his electoral victory. His parrot phrases were 'the young country' and 'new Britain'. He told *Vanity Fair*: 'I'm delighted at the success of British pop music. And fashion and design are tremendously important. We're providing really high-quality goods and ideas that the world wants to buy.'

And when, in his 1996 conference speech, Blair ended by paying homage to the Euro '96 Baddiel, Skinner and Lightning Seeds/Broudie football anthem, with the phrase, 'Seventeen years of hurt never stopped us dreaming ... Labour's coming home', it was kinda cool at the time. As Williams said, 'This sounded like proper, conviction politics, the kind that people will die for (in peace marches, not imperialist wars, silly). Conviction is always cool.'

'This is a new age, to be led by a new generation,' Blair went on. 'Together, we [can] make this the young country of my generation's dreams.'

The fact is—and this is not to decry the achievements of the government, such as the minimum wage and Northern Ireland's continued peace process success—its obsession with youth created the most right-wing Labour Party the movement has known.

Why is Blair so uncool now? To take some examples at random from his recent bad press—receiving a far-right American president hospitably, blagging free holidays while nurses are denied free holidays offered by patients as an abuse of their position, giving less than sufficient charity donations (which, anyway, he can offset against tax with some fat cat creative accounting).

But the uncoolest thing he did was the attack on Iraq. Nothing could be less cool than a Labour government, yes a *Labour* government, siding with the Bush family against the rest of the world. It has been a cool con trick. In May 1997 when Blair's Labour government swept to power, Britain was declared the coolest place on the planet: art, pop, nightlife and politics seemed young, not so dumb, and full of come. Then what happened? The obsession with youth became mock radicalism hiding conservatism, art became a cloak for naked materialism, and our full-of-hope Labour government made an alliance with the Bush family to go to war in Iraq and young energetic Blair had heart problems at 50. The media were sold a pup.

Just as people are increasingly cynical and apathetic about politicians like Blair and the current crisis of representation, it seems nowadays British newspapers are trusted by their readers far less than any others in the European Union, according to evidence published by Eurobarometer, the polling arm of the European Commission. With this decline in popular journalism, to paraphrase Orwell, if there's any hope for informed, honest and humane reporting in mass circulation papers, it lies with those like the *Daily Mirror*, providing it doesn't succumb to the pro-Blair line. As for the majority of today's downmarket media, they—like Tony Blair—should have stayed an Ugly Rumour.

Appendix

Portrait of the journalist as a consumer

Books
Brighton Rock—Graham Greene
Platinum Logic—Tony Parsons
Tough Tough Toys for Tough Tough Boys—Will Self
Love It or Shove It—Julie Burchill
The New Journalism—Tom Wolfe
Backlash—Susan Faludi
Heroes—John Pilger
The Ragged Trousered Philanthopists—Robert Tressell
The Lion and the Unicorn—George Orwell
The Scholar—Courttia Newland

Records
What's Happening Brother?—Marvin Gaye
It's Alright Now—Eddie Harris
Penitentiary Philosophy—Erykah Badu
In Da Club—50 Cent
Message to the messagers—Gil Scott Heron
Tutti Frutti—Little Richard
People Get Ready—The Impressions
Angel—Jimi Hendrix
The Beat Of Hostile Street—Anti Social Workers vs the Mad Professor
The Whole Point of No Return—The Style Council

Films
Mean Streets
Performance
Manhattan
Kids
Blue Collar
On the Waterfront
Animal House
Bowling for Columbine
Do the Right Thing
Bread and Roses

TV
Bilko
Law and Order
Only Fools and Horses
Life on Earth
Till Death Us Do Part
Frasier
Sopranos
Cheers
Roseanne
The Simpsons

Radio
Today Programme
Dead Ringers
Norman Jay on Radio London
Matt White's *Smooth Grooves* on Kiss
Trevor Nelson on Radio 1
Jonathan Ross on Radio 2
Westwood (when on LWR)
Jigs on Choice FM
Lisa l'Anson show on Radio London
John Peel on Radio 1

Style
The Duffer of St George
Agnes B
Camden Market
Paul Smith
Alexander McQueen
Browns
Soul II Soul
Lillywhites
Daks
Black Market

People
AJP Taylor
Billie Holiday
GF Newman
Muhammad Ali
Dennis Skinner
Ms Dynamite
Johnny Vaughan
Richard Pryor
Bob Woodward
Tracey Emin

Clubs
Electric Ballroom, Camden
People's Club, Paddington
Lacey Lady, Ilford
Ministry of Sound, Elephant & Castle
Bass Clef, Hoxton
Africa Centre, Covent Garden
Pacha, Ibiza
Hacienda, Manchester
Wigan Casino
Gossips/The Wag, Soho

From World's End to World War
A socialist serviceman's story

ALF GOLDBERG
Foreword by TONY BENN

'...truly wonderful...a splendid combination of wit and precision...in a different class...' — *Tony Benn*

'...admirable...an excellent example of history written from the bottom up' — *Tribune*

'Moving accounts of solidarity and camaraderie...combines humour, tragedy and social comment' — *Labour Left Briefing*

'Wartime Blackpool is vividly recreated...' — *Lancashire Life*

'...details the everyday lives of the working class under conditions of war...' — *The Big Issue in the North*

'...vividly captures the atmosphere of wartime Blackpool and the Fylde...' — *The Gazette*, Blackpool

'...gives a socialist slant on the Second World War...' — *Lytham St Annes Express*

From World's End to World War is available from The Progressive Press, 3 June Avenue, Blackpool FY4 4LQ. E-mail: barrymac@ukip.co.uk

Hardback, 168 pages, £7.95 including p&p. ISBN 0 9546121 0 8.